AMAZON

FBA

MASTERY COACHING &

PASSIVE

INCOME

THE HOLY GRAIL OF
FINANCIAL FREEDOM

JONATHAN FITZPATRICK

AMAZON FBA MASTERY COACHING & PASSIVE INCOME
Copyright © 2019 by Jonathan Fitzpatrick.

For information contact :
Suite #K231125
13820 NE Airport Way
Portland, OR, 97251
United States

info@jonathanfitzpatrickauthor.com

www.jonathanfitzpatrickauthor.com

www.facebook.com/jonathanfitzpatrickauthor

First Edition : October 2019

DISCLAIMER

The information contained in this book is for general information and educational purposes only.
This book assumes no responsibility for errors or omissions in the contents on the Service.

This book have no liability for any damage or loss (including, without limitation, financial loss, loss of profits, loss of business or any indirect or consequential loss).

 JONATHAN FITZPATRICK

SIGN UP!

Visit our website
WWW.JONATHANFITZPATRICKAUTHOR.COM
and enter you email address to receive exclusive bonus contents related to the updates of this book and find out everything about Jonathan Fitzpatrick's new publications, launch offers and other exclusive promotions!

CONTENTS

THE DEFINITIVE GUIDE TO LEARN THE SECRET
WAY TO SELL FULFILLMENT BY AMAZON

AMAZON
FBA MASTERY
COACHING

How to Launch a Private Label and Earn
Six Figures of Passive Income in an
Easy Step-By-Step Method from
Total Beginners to Really Advanced

JONATHAN FITZPATRICK

INTRODUCTION

My name is Jonathan Fitzpatrick and I am an online entrepreneur. In my first 12 months of business, I was able to go from earning $0 to earning six-figures of passive income through Amazon FBA. Now I want to share my knowledge and experience with others so that they can also reach their full potential. Learn how to launch a private label and earn six-figures of passive income in just twelve months! This comprehensive guide applies whether you are an experienced seller or just getting started.

I'm writing this introduction from the first-class cabin of a flight bound for Tokyo as it is going to be a long flight, and I intend to make the best out of my time. Whether you take me for my word, or not, I can assure you that this vacation is entirely funded by my FBA account. While still on vacation, I will still be running my business if necessary. It completely runs on my smart phone, laptop and sometimes the barcode scanner.

More so, you would be envious of the amount of freedom I have to juggle and balance my personal and professional life. When was the last time I did something I love and enjoy? Well, I currently am. I love writing and disseminating knowledge. But if you are speaking in the realms of hobbies, then you should know that I do not miss any of my evening book club sessions. In fact, just yesterday afternoon I managed to attend a painting class, grab a drink with a friend and still managed to be home on time to read my niece a bedtime story. I believe that now I have your undivided attention.

These are the perks that have come with FBA. Fulfillment By Amazon. This is the gold mine that is little understood by those who know about it, let alone less publicized to the general public. For those who are quite familiar with the service, they understand that it is as simple as Buy; Ship; Receive Payment. Then why is it so complicated if it seems as natural.

Well, truth be told, FBA is rather intensive. Regardless of Amazon handling a huge chunk of the program, the bit left to the sellers is not a walk in the park. But I suppose that you already know this, and that is precisely why you are here. You understand what it takes to achieve your financial goals. With your primary goals set out, it will be a far easier job wading through these waters. Add that to an active and fueled mindset and a prosperous story is already being penned.

This book is meant to give an in depth understanding of Fulfillment By Amazon and how to reap maximum benefits from it. It provides instructions and guidelines for managing an FBA business as well as tips to give you an edge over your competition. I have learned most of the practices through research, experimentation, trial, and error, consulting other FBA sellers and personally through patience. FBA, the book, has been compiled to help you achieve success through Amazon. Do you wish to make a couple of thousand dollars in monthly profits? Well, roll up your sleeves, it is time for business.

Tip: I would like you to take a moment and reflect on your mindset. It is the one thing that will keep you going. Set it right, and no obstacle will deter you from that handsome Amazon deposit in your bank account.

CHAPTER 1
FBA BASICS

ulfillment by Amazon (FBA) is often considered a subset of the dropshipping industry with a few major differences. Whereas with traditional dropshipping a third party is responsible for the sourcing and fulfilment of the orders, merchants in a Fulfilment by Amazon relationship send their items to Amazon who is then responsible for storing and shipping the items in question in return for a portion of the profits from the sale of the item. If you have an item that you are interested in creating a private label for but you weren't sure where the items were going to be stored or how you were going to find time to fill all of your future orders, then FBA is the answer.

In addition to making the physical transaction part of an online sale much less of a hassle, those who participate in the FBA program also get preferential treatment when it comes to search results as well as how their packages are shipped. Amazon power users who take advantage of the Amazon Prime membership option receive free 2-day shipping on countless products that Amazon sells directly, but also, on all of the items sold by those in the FBA program.

This means that by simply signing up for FBA you are already placing your future products at a huge advantage when compared to similar products that you will one day be competing against. The amount you are charging for shipping will also affect your Amazon rating in several ways, but suffice it to say, a lower shipping cost is always better. This, coupled with 2-day shipping, goes a long way towards creating positive mindshare, even if your product costs a little more, or is of a new private label brand that the customer has not yet heard of.

HOW IT WORKS
FBA works by allowing sellers to send their products directly to the nearest Amazon fulfilment facility where the products are then stored until they are sold. You then have the option of paying for additional preparation or labeling services as required while paying a monthly storage fee based on the amount of space your products require. Then, once a customer finds them online, Amazon takes care of all of the fulfilment tasks, including the all-important customer service and returns portion of the process which a more traditional dropshipping service would leave up to you.

It is important to understand just how valuable the fact that Amazon is fulfilling the orders in question is, especially when it comes to private label products from a new company. The Amazon name carries quite a bit of weight with customers, and having that name involved in the transaction will make them much more likely to go ahead and pull the trigger on the transaction in question. While they will hopefully become a loyal follower of your brand someday, being an FBA member gets you in the door. Studies show that FBA sellers typically see as much as a 30 percent boost in sales compared to more traditional sellers.

In return for the perks, FBA members pay a $40 monthly fee as well as a percentage of the sale price of each item. You will also be required to pay fees related to the weight of the item when it comes to shipping, any handling fees, pack or pick fees and storage fees based on the square footage. Additionally, you will be required to pay fees related to individually labeling all of your products as you will not want them commingled with other similar products as this will only dilute your brand. If you are unsure if this fee structure will fit the private label products, you may be hoping to one day sell you can check out the revenue calculator available on the official FBA site to determine if your idea is likely going to be a success.

When it comes to fleshing out your business plan it is important to factor in the benefits in terms of exposure that you will likely receive as well as any costs you might incur. This is especially true if you are going to be creating your own product line as you are going to need all of the potential customers you can get. If your initial idea does not appear as though it is going to work with FBA, you may want to consider alternative types of products as the solution is out there, you just have to do the work and find it.

A private label brand is any brand that it is not owned by a major company or organization. Over the past 20 years, private label brands have seen nearly double the growth of more mainstream brands, and the growth in niche markets where the importance of individual ingredient lists is much higher; much like customer interest levels when it comes to getting to know the creators of unique brands.

This is in large part due to the greater amount of perceived control that goes along with these types of products and it is something you can use to your advantage if marketed properly. What's more, when you decide to create your own private label you will have complete control over the branding and marketing of the product in question, allowing you to create something truly special that speaks directly to your target audience. Additionally, you will have the added advantage of perceived value as you don't have to deal with all of the added waste that comes from working with a major brand.

THE PRODUCT

For me personally, this is the most difficult part of starting a business. The beginning. The foundation, perhaps. Knowing what to sell to people is like knowing the exact shirt and tie combination to wear for a specific job interview. A polished cover letter and rehearsed answers for the interviewer's questions are far less effective if you dress inappropriately. Too casual is disrespectful and too formal makes you look desperate.

The items you choose to sell to people say something about you. Regardless of whether or not you have any practical use for the product, your signature will be all over them (sometimes literally). The material quality, the packaging, the storage conditions, the handling. While a one-time customer may not notice a lot of those things, a regular customer will likely be looking at all of those things and more.

Choosing a product: If you did not start your business with a creative idea of your own already in mind then you will need to look for an opportunity. Any of the following is a great place to start
- Opportunities in Keywords
- Building an Interesting Brand
- Identify and Solve a Pain Point
- Identify and Cater to Passions
- Look for an Opportunity Gap
- Utilize Your Own Experience
- Capitalize on Trends
- Opportunities in Keywords

Keywords: Starting from the top, we have opportunities derived from search engine keywords. Keywords are the words and phrases that users type into a search engine. Knowing a little bit about search engine optimization (SEO) is essential if you want to be competitive online. A lot of business owners are willing to handsomely pay savvy individuals to manage their advertising campaigns.

Anyway, the idea here is to find keywords that have a high search volume (a lot of people looking for it) and low competition (few good matches). That right there is a golden opportunity. Giving the people something that they already want means you can launch with a smaller ad campaign than if you were trying to get into a competitive market.

Building an interesting brand: A popular strategy for entering a saturated and/or competitive market, as the 'new kid on the block' you have less money, less influence, and less experience than the older boys. Trying to keep up with them is an almost futile act. You need something unique. Something that only you have that makes others pay attention to you even if you are a rookie in a room full of champions and veterans. This is your brand.

I could list some specific examples but there are just so many! I suppose one of the most well-known is Apple's more stylish branding being used to separate their products from Microsoft's dull ones. Even a Goliath like Microsoft is not safe from an opponent who knows how to stand out from the rest.

You can take the same route as Apple and distinguish your brand visually. You could also just tell your own story. Few consumers think about the people behind brands like Wal-Mart or McDonald's. Instead, they think of how huge those businesses are and how rich the owners and executives must be. Highlighting your status as a small business without a lot of capital can make you far more relatable to the average shopper.

Identify and solve a pain point: There has never been a better time to be alive in history. The best and brightest of us have worked diligently to make every one of us live comfortably. Once deadly diseases are now treatable if not curable. Modern vehicles make travel so easy that plans are being made to explore the solar system. Advancing technology continues to make performing tasks so easy that people are afraid of not having jobs in the near future.

All of the things that cause discomfort are pain points. I mentioned some big ones but there are small ones, too. I can type out this book on a computer because dipping pens in ink that smudged all over the paper was a pain point for writers. The printing press and typewriters were revolutionary even though they were not cures for cancer. Try isolating some minor frustrations and then think of products that can remove them.

Note that when I brought up advancing technology, I also included a fear that people have. The solution to what was once a problem can create a new problem. Be on the lookout for innovations that change the way a lot of us live. Those changes can create an environment for a new pain point to develop.

Identify and cater to passions: I think this type of opportunity is the easiest to understand. You identify something that a lot of people are interested and provide an additional something that appeals to those people. This is what many people do with blogs and vlogs to start building a following. Someone who wants to travel but is unable to will settle for a virtual escape in the meantime.

Fan merchandise falls under this category, too. You should get permission before reproducing symbols and logos that belong to someone else, but fan art can be sold legally as of the time that I am writing this. If you are an artist, slap that art onto clothes, mugs, and bags if you think the fanatics will buy them.

Not an artist? Well somebody has to supply all the clothes, mugs, and bags to be printed over. Creative types are all about that passion and you can take advantage of that. It is also possible that one person can do all of the above. If you share the same passion as your clients then a lot of this work could feel more like an addictive hobby. Cater responsibly.

Look for an opportunity gap: As smartphones became ubiquitous in the early 2000s, the people ran into a problem. They wanted to take photos of themselves using their phones. However, it was near impossible to get the right angle and lighting while holding the device only an arm's length away. Friendly bystanders were a godsend but could not be relied upon at all times. The people cried out for a solution and the market answered their cries with the Selfie Stick.

That is how you take advantage of an opportunity gap. Human beings always want 'more' regardless of how much they already have. People in houses want bigger houses. People who own a car want another car. People who get food delivered to their homes want faster delivery. There will always be a demand for something new to make living just a little bit easier. Provide something to achieve that goal and you will have plenty of business.

Opportunity gaps are like minor pain points; nobody complains because they are more of an inconvenience than a cause of stress. Discovering one will take research and awareness. You can ask the people around you about the products they use and if they feel like something is missing when they use them.

Utilize your own experience: Young entrepreneurs are still young people. They are optimistic and ambitious with little to lose and so much to gain. Older people tend to move with caution and lower expectations. One of your biggest assets, as you age, is your experience. Wisdom cannot be bought or stolen and its value is priceless.

The more work experience and expertise you have in a field, the more of an advantage you have others who are entering it. Writing and publishing your own book should not only generate some income but also show others in the field that you know what you are talking about. As a consequence of that, any products you sell in the future will stand out because of your reputation.

Your choice of media does not have to be in writing. You can make videos or host seminars. The objective is just to make it known that you are an authority in your field. Not feeling confident? Do it regardless! If even one of your industry insights is unique it might be enough to establish a following.

Capitalize on trends: This one is tricky. The idea is similar to that of finding opportunities in keywords. A trend has to be identified early and capitalized on immediately for the best results. Being the second person to catch on might not be good enough depending on consumer demand and how long the trend lasts.
Let us pretend that I have identified what I believe to be a trend. How do I confirm this? The most straightforward way is to buy a small amount of whatever I think I need to sell and put it up for sale.

If sales are anything less than stellar then either I am too late or I have not identified a trend at all. If it really is trendy, I should see a significant amount of that product sold in a couple of days. The next step is to buy a lot more of that trendy product and make sure consumers know what I have done so.

CONSIDER DIFFERENT TYPES OF PRODUCTS

For starters, you are going to want to ensure that the first products in your inaugural product line are durable enough to stand up to a bumpy delivery process as nothing will ruin your ratings like numerous reviews talking about how their purchases arrived broken

---

Choose the right items: While it is natural to consider big ticket items to flip as an easy way of generating a major payout, the fact of the matter is that you are almost always going to have more luck selling numerous small items than you will selling one large item. The best place to start is with common, everyday items that you know someone, somewhere is sure to need.

The goal here should be to choose items that are always going to be in demand, but not those that are so vital as to ensure that most people are likely to run out and buy it the second they need it, no matter what the circumstances. While not the most exciting advice, give it a try and you will see that a hefty supply of printer cartridges or diapers can be worth their long-term weight in gold.

While certain items are going to be worthwhile investments no matter what the situation, others can be sure to generate massive windfalls if picked up for the right price to start with. A great example of this is holiday decorations as they can easily be picked up for bargain basement pricing starting the day after the holiday in question has passed. Keep in mind, however, that you can only realistically expect to make a profit on these types of items if you have the time and inclination to hold on to them until the next year when that holiday once again rolls around. Alternatively, you can keep up to date on the bleeding edge of cool and purchase items that are sure to be in high demand six months down the line for much more reasonable prices.

Choosing the right items to sell also means considering all facets of the items in question, including how easy they will ultimately be to ship once you do, in fact, make a sale. Failing to do so leaves you open to the possibility of having to deal with a large number of returns on items that are needlessly fragile. Along similar lines, it is also extremely important to consider the overall weight of the item in question to ensure that shipping costs aren't going to be eating up too much of your profit as well as any issues if you are going to ship the product internationally.

START SELLING

Now that you are ready, it is time to go to Amazon and set up your seller account. To begin with, you should set up a free Individual Seller Plan. As you do this, you will want to be sure that you are verifying your account information. Before we go over upgrading to FBA, we suggest understanding the difference between the selling plans. This may sway your thoughts on joining FBA.

Individual Selling Plan
- $0.99 for each item that sells on Amazon
- Only one listing at a time
- Includes both online listings as well as the management of your orders
- Includes Seller Central tools to help with account functions

Professional Selling Plan
- Costs a Monthly Fee of $39.99
- Get multiple listings by using uploads and spreadsheets
- Includes reports and fees on your inventory and management of orders
- Includes access to the Amazon Marketplace Web Service, API functions, and daily reports on your store's performance.

If you decide that FBA is the proper choice for your store, you can quickly switch your selling plan. To begin, you will want to click on the tab that says 'Seller Account.' Once you have done this, tap on the settings button and click 'Account Info.' Under this tab, it will ask you to click a button that says 'Modify Plan.' Once you are here, you will be able to upgrade your plan, and you are all set to go! The program processes immediately. It should be noted that you will be charged a $0.99 fee for any orders that you close. From this point on, you will be charged $39.99 a month as long as you keep the Professional plan.

Amazon Seller's Application: The first thing that you will want to do is to download the seller application available from Amazon directly. This application is extremely useful as it allows you to put in the details of any product you are thinking about selling to learn how much you will make off of the item at a set price minus all the various fees that will come along with it. What's more, this application will allow you to see how many other people are currently selling the same item, as well as which varieties of a given brand are the most popular among consumers at the current point in time.

CamelCamelCamel.com: This website and other like it allow you to find out more detailed information regarding how a specific product is currently doing on Amazon. These types of sites provide you with the data that you will need to not only determine if the price an item is currently selling for is on the high or low end of the spectrum, it will show you the entire history of that item so you know if you have found an emerging trend or have latched on to a product that is past its prime. Checking out this site or other like it, before you set your prices, is extremely important to ensure you aren't accidentally selling yourself, and your items, short.

LISTING ITEMS
When it comes to listing the items that you have worked so hard to create or buy for a price that you can turn a profit on the first thing you are going to want to do is find the Inventory option at the top of the page in the Amazon Seller Central page. From there all you need to do is select the option to add a product. After this, you will want to select the option to create a new product which will require the use of a unique UPC code as well as an AISN number, the specifics of which can be found below.

After you have created the item that you are planning to list, you will be asked 3 important questions. First you will need to set a price for the item, then you will need to describe the condition of the items you are selling and finally, you will want to choose the Fulfilment by Amazon option which is listed as wanting Amazon to take care of shipping. When it comes to choosing a price for your products, a good rule of thumb is to start out by looking at similar products in your niche and then setting a comparative price. It is important to take into account your costs as well, as underselling the competition won't do any good if you aren't making a profit in the long run.

Creating a shipping plan: After you have finished loading in all of your products, you will want to choose the option to Send Inventory on the final product. This will lead to a prompt to create a shipping plan which includes choosing a shipping address and packaging type. Packaging type can be split into 2 different categories, individual products or case-packed products. In general, you are likely going to want to select case-packed products which indicates that all of the items in each box are the same. Shipping your products in groups will save you plenty of logistical headaches in the long run and is always recommended.

After you have finished choosing your shipping plan you will be prompted to determine which items you are going to be shipping at this time. Adding products to the shipment is as easy as clicking the add product button. If you find yourself in need of adding additional items, simply post them as normal before selecting the option to add the item to an existing plan.

_____

Shipping your items: Once you have all of the items added to the shipping plan in question you will want to go back to the main Seller Central page before selecting the option for Inventory. From there you will want to select the option to "continue shipping plan" where you will be able to list how many of each product you are going to be sending. If your product is going to require some type of preparation prior to being sent to customers this is also where you make it clear what all you are going to need Amazon to do to get them ready to ship.

You will also need to reconfirm that you are going to require labeling services before being asked to set the weight of the package or packages in question. This doesn't need to be exact, as long as you estimate over what you know the weight to be. This can quickly become costly, however, so investing in a package scale is recommended.

From there it is simply a matter of boxing up your products, printing out the provided shipping labels and dropping the boxes off at a local UPS location. Your products will be listed live as soon as they reach the nearest Amazon fulfillment office and then it will be up to your ancillary marketing activities as well as your becoming an authority, discussed in the next chapter, to get your products sold as quickly as possible.

Subscriptions: Amazon subscriptions are new to Amazon and they were launched in order to help customers save money and for sellers to get more money. With this, you are going to get a discount because there are going to be a variety of products that are going to arrive on the customer's doorstep on a schedule.

This helps to convince customers, since items that they need to buy regularly are going to be sent to their store and this makes it to where they do not have to worry about going to the warehouse and the store not having the brand that they want or the see that the price has gone up without them knowing.

Like anything else on Amazon, the product that you have to sell is going to have to comply with the rules of Amazon as well as the rules and regulations of the territory that you are in. These rules and regulations are in place to ensure that the customers and the sellers are protected.

Not only do you have the option of doing a subscription that is delivered to the customer's door, but you can do subscriptions on Amazon Prime, Amazon TV, and Kindle Unlimited. All of these are brilliant strategies to use when selling the product that you have to offer. It all depends on what you are selling.

CHAPTER 2
CHOOSE THE RIGHT NICHE

When it comes to ensuring you are ultimately able to market the products you eventually sell as effectively as possible the first, and perhaps most important, thing that you will need to consider is what niche of the market you are going to cater to. A niche is a specialized section of the larger consumer market as a whole which naturally lends itself to a specific set of customer demographics as well as products and interests. For example, the online dating market is a broad category which holds several different niches including things like polyamory, green dating, sacred sexuality, soulmates and more. These niches can then  be broken down even further into things such as polyamory over 40 or homosexual sacred sexuality.

Choosing a specialized niche is a great way to help yourself stick out from the crowd and, in so doing, making your FBA business that much more profitable in the long run. This is easier said than done, however, as not every niche or sub-niche is going to be profitable for one reason or another which is why it is so important to do the proper research before you begin. Remember, once you have branded your store with a specific niche it can be extremely difficult to change it later on.

The best way to make a lot of money is for your niche to be something you care about enough to go back to every day. This is going to drive you to work on it and constantly produce something new. If you don't care about your niche then it's going to show through in your posts. You can expect some amount of return, but they will almost certainly not be great. Bear that in mind as you go forward.

So, you've gotten to the point now that you want to start considering an FBA business in a serious way then the first thing that you're going to need to do is pick your niche. There are two ways to go about doing this.

The first is the hardest: go off of your passions. If you do this, you're going to have to find innovative ways using products that affiliate companies offer, if they don't have any for your specific niche. However, this can pay off by you making really creative and potentially viral posts using things in unconventional ways that people will see as super intriguing. This is a good way to bring in a whole bunch of people.

In order to do this, you're going to need to be very crafty and keep an eye on what's available. Additionally, a lot of your income will be coming through other means mentioned in this book rather than affiliate marketing. However, it's an option worth considering because affiliate marketing can almost certainly play a part in a strategy like this one.

The second is the easiest, but you're playing chance in two respects. The second method is to simply see what products and avenues are available to you through affiliate marketing channels and then derive your niche from that. In some cases, this will intertwine with the first concept and you'll find something that you're both passionate about and that there are a fair number of products for which you can market. However, this won't always be the case.

In the event that you can't find something you're reasonably passionate about, simply try to find something that you're somewhat interested in or would like to learn more about for yourself. This will make it easier to research and find topics related to it that you're interested in.

However, sometimes you just won't be able to find anything that interests you. In these cases, you can still just go with whatever you think would do fairly well. Sometimes intuition can be a really important thing, and in these cases, you should just trust your intuition in trying to find a pertinent niche through affiliate marketing channels.

The last and third most prominent way to figure out your niche is simply to use keywords in order to learn what topics are hot right now. This might give you the most instantaneous benefit, but you will inevitably find it rather difficult to carry this out for a long period of time because trends are constantly changing. You'll most likely find success using this method in the short run (if you can write some great articles and take advantage of available affiliate marketing opportunities) but you'll find it difficult to maintain that same level of success in the long run.

If you do decide to take this avenue, however, all you'll have to do is get access to popular keywords and figure out what's trending. The easiest way to do this is probably to take advantage of Google Trends. Simply Google "google trends hot trends" and the page you're looking for should be relatively easy to find. This will tell you the most trending topics of the day every hour or so. It's generally the top 20.

However, this can be rather unwieldy as it won't exactly tell you the sort of information you're wanting to write a book about. After all, these are just the most trending searches for the last day or so, and they generally on very specific people and events rather than topics you can easily write a book about.

NARROWING DOWN A NICHE

Choose the right target: When it comes to finding the best possible niche or subniche for you, the first thing you are going to want to consider is who your ideal target audience is going to be. There are several different options when it comes to choosing the right audience, starting with choosing the one of which you are currently a part. This has the added bonus of ensuring you don't have to do excessive research to get started and will also ensure that you have the interest required to stick with it in the long-term.

Alternately, you could choose a niche that you are just starting to become more interested in, though in doing so you run the risk of losing interest in the topic and being stuck with a blog you are loath to update. If you can't seem to come up with the right audience, but you have a niche in mind then you can simply start with the niche and seek out an audience based on the ideal characteristic, discretionary spending.

Learn more about them: Once you have a target audience in mind, the next thing you are going to need to do is to think about all of the problems, challenges, pain points, aspirations and desires that your target audience likely deals with on a regular basis and how you can make this process easier for them in as many different ways as possible. A good place to go for research at this juncture is a basic Google search as if you put in problems your target audience deals with you will find searches revolving around ways to solve the problem. Without a problem to solve, the target audience will likely need to buy far less than they otherwise would.

Find the profit: After you find a few problems that people are regularly looking to solve, the next thing you are going to want to do is to determine which are going to be the most profitable from an affiliate marketing standpoint. The best way to do so is going to be by going to Adwords.Google.com and looking up the keyword planning tool. This tool will allow you to filter the search results you see to just those that you are interested in before searching for both local and global results.

Determine if anything is going to set you apart from the pack: Depending on what you find during your initial fact finding mission your next step will need to be figuring out just what is going to set you and your products apart from all of the other stores that are offering similar, if not the same product. What this typically comes down to is how much personality or added value you can add to your store, to the point that it makes it preferable for customers to seek you out instead of simply settling for a generic version and calling it a day.

People seek out niche options despite the fact that Amazon sells practically everything because they like knowing they are directly connecting with another person and because they are looking for a little extra personality in their purchased goods. If you can't afford to throw in additional incentives, consider specializing in a few items to a degree that other stores, even your competitors, can't match. Regardless of how specific your competitors might be, there is general a way to be more specialized, consider the market from other perspectives and you will find your own way to shine.

Check out magazines: While magazines largely make their money through the subscriptions that their readers pay, another essential way that these magazines make their money is through the products that they promote. For example, if you have ever flipped through a magazine and have thought that there are far too many advertisements in it, then it is safe to say that the magazine that you are looking gets a lot of money from the advertisements that they feature. While this fact may mean that you have too many pages to flip through to get to some readable content, it also means that from a research perspective, this magazine may benefit you more than you think. Remember, these advertisers would not be buying ad spots in magazines if they did not think that the ads would lead to sales.

Another important tip that goes along with looking through the advertisements that you see in ads is to be on the lookout for ads that are enticing to you personally. While yes, a business should be as emotionless as possible, your dropshipping business should also sell products about which you are somewhat passionate. For example, if you decide that you are going to sell tires online because your research suggests that they will sell well, but you hate cars in general, then this may not be the best option for you. If you can find a happy medium between a product that will profitable and a product that you will also enjoy selling, that would be ideal. Of course, if your goal is to make as much money as you can, then this advice may be lost on you; however, it can be argued that enjoying what you are doing should be a part of any business endeavor that you take on.

Check on the competition: Once you have an idea of what items are in need in the niche, your next step should be to determine the level of competition when it comes to specific item types. The more online stores that you find selling the same product or variations thereon the more direct competition you will have when it comes time to actually start selling products. You can find more than 2 pages of search results selling the items you are thinking about selling with no more than a basic search you may want to consider a different niche or at least targeting a sub-niche to carve out more of a unique audience.

While checking out the competition you will want to do all of the reconnaissance to ensure that you have a good idea of what their product turnover seems to be and how robust their customer base seems to be. While scouting out the competition it is important to approach them in a rational fashion and not set out determined to crush them no matter what. At this point is likely a better choice to cut your losses and find another niche before you start putting real time and effort into this one; remember, discretion is the better part of valor.

Additionally, you will want to consider the strength of any obvious competitor's social media campaigns and search engine optimization SEO. To determine how popular and effective each is, you simply need to do basic searches with terms related to the niche you are interested in infiltrating. If a few names keep coming up again and again and again, then you may want to consider looking for a new product to sell.

Maintain perspective: If your first niche ends up looking as though it is already as crowded enough as it is, then it is important to not stay married to an idea that you have absolutely no investment in at this point. It is much better to find out that your first choice ended up not being as viable as you thought in the planning stage rather than when you have already made a significant investment into making your online store a reality. Maintain the right perspective and be ready to walk away up to the point that your website is live and ready to receive customers.

Consider the quality: When it comes to finding ways to set yourself apart from the competition, one of the best ways of doing so is by offering a better quality of product for relatively the same price. Depending on the types of items you are selling, being known for quality is more important than anything save an extreme price difference.

When given a choice the average consumer is likely to put quality first in terms of importance which is why you must ensure that whatever you end up selling you do whatever you need to in order to ensure that the quality of every product that your store sells be as high as possible. While it may be tempting to reduce your costs as thoroughly as possible early on, in reality, this is less of an investment in the future and more of a guarantee that your first customers could be your only customers. A reputation for quality will spread quickly and can do more for a fledgling startup than just about any other marketing tool.

CHAPTER 3
PRODUCTS

Once you have gone ahead and chosen what niche you want to fill, the next thing you need to do is determine what you want to sell. Deciding what you sell is extremely important as it will influence the type of marketing you will want to try further down the line and also determine where you can go to source the things you want to sell. In general, you want items that are specific enough to not already have thousands of online stores already filling the niche, while at the same time broad enough to still see traffic from general Google searches. The right mix can be tricky, but you'll know it when you find it.

Consider the demand: One of the first things you will want to consider is whether you have the knowledge about your chosen niche that is currently being underserved by the online community. For example, if you really enjoy knitting and know that alpaca wool yarn is the best, then consider selling it if it is relatively hard to find currently. Everyone is part of a niche if you try hard enough, take the time to think about the items you buy regularly that are either hard to find or wear out extremely quickly, it can help to write the ideas down as you think of them, so you don't need to work through the entire process with each, ruining your brainstorming flow.

Once you have a list of ideas, the next step is to assess the relative demand for each of the potential items in question. As long as the items you are thinking about selling aren't extremely obscure, this process should be relatively straightforward. A good way to start researching the popularity of a specific item is to simply type it into the Google search bar and see what options appear under the autofill option. Again, what you are looking for here is a demand that is not being entirely met, so questions about where to find specific items are a great positive unmet desire indicator.

PRIVATE LABEL BASICS

When it comes to creating your own private label there are a few things you are going to want to keep in mind to ensure you get into the private label FBA business with the proper mindset. This means that the first thing you need to consider is the amount of capital that it is going to require in order to create your initial product line. It requires a significant amount of capital to get your own private label up and running and the larger or more complicated your product is the greater those expenses are going to be. If you are interested in getting started selling on Amazon on the cheap, retail arbitrage is more your speed, to create a private label you have to be willing to spend.

The next thing you need to understand is that creating a private label is not going to make you large amounts of money in a fashion that is either quick or easy. Instead, it is going to take lots of hard work and dedication and be unlikely to pay off realistically for anywhere between 6 months and a year depending on various factors related to the niche you ultimately chose. For those who choose to stick it out, however, the rewards are substantial. Not only will you have a fully functioning brand operating exclusively through Amazon but you will have something that businesses all around the world are constantly striving for, brand recognition, and it will be yours and yours alone.

Deciding if your product is a good fit for a private label: Once you've done some research and determined what niche is going to likely be a good fit for you, the next thing you are going to want to consider is if the market is favorable when it comes to private labels. The first thing this means is determining if there is one or more national brand in the niche space that already dominates the space. This means you will naturally be limited in what you can choose, though you can likely find a sub niche that is more agreeable to private labels if you try hard enough.

Design the right logo: When it comes to designing a logo, it is important to consider what you ultimately go with long and hard as your logo is going to be seen more than any other aspect of your business. When it comes to finding the right logo for you, a good place to start is with common symbols as when done properly your logo will spring to mind whenever that symbol is used. When thinking about your logo it is important to consider how it looks when it is the size of a thumbnail as it is when it is filling your screen completely. You never know where your logo might end up and it is important to plan accordingly. Likewise, it is important to pick a logo that can default to colors that resemble the colors of your store but it should be just as recognizable when any other colors are inserted into the mix.

When choosing a logo, it is important to pick something that is timeless instead of cashing in on a current trend. While a trendy logo might get you some notice today, it is much more likely to be a hindrance in the long run. Create a logo that you are sure will be comfortable with for the foreseeable future.

When it comes to choosing the colors, the first thing you should consider is a few core colors that complement one another as well as few more colors that are variations on the first. It is important to keep the color variation to a minimum as simple, clean looks are currently in fashion. Certain colors are also known to stimulate certain responses which make them natural choices when it comes to selling certain products.

Choosing a name: While it doesn't take much to pick out a bad company name when you see it, understand what it takes to create a good name can be much more complicated. To get started, you may want to consider which of the three primary name conventions, whimsical, evocative or descriptive, that you want to explore more fully. Descriptive names are self-explanatory, much like the names themselves and include things like Office Depot, Bed, Bath and Beyond and Home Depot. Alternately you can go with something that is evocative without really being descriptive such as Warby Parker or Oracle. Finally, you may want to consider something that's catchy without being meaningful such as Twitter, Google or Hulu.

Know what's popular: When it comes to creating a useful business name, it will automatically make it easier for you to attract new customers if people can find your business by simply searching for whatever product or service it is that you provide. The best way to go about picking out the optimal search terms for your product or service is to utilize the website UberSuggest.org. All you need to do is enter any word into its search bar and it will provide you with all of the most popular search terms related to it.

Consider related words: If you don't have anything catchy in mind right off the bat, the first thing you are going to want to consider is words that are naturally related to the product or service that you want to provide. A thesaurus of either the physical or digital sort is a great place to start and you never know when a new word might spark the creative notion that gives birth to your new business name. If nothing jumps out at you right from the start, simply make a list of between 50 and 100 potential options and save them for later.

PRODUCT MANUFACTURING
This section applies to those of you who want to make your own products or even have an invention manufactured.

Prototype: The first step in the manufacturing process is to create a prototype. The prototype is going to be the preliminary model of the product that you want to be made in bulk. If you are creating something mechanical then the prototype has to be able to function exactly as you want it to. Otherwise, you could manufacture hundreds of models that are effectively overpriced paperweights.

It is safe to say that creating your own style of t-shirt is different from re-inventing the electric oven.

Some prototypes are things that you can make yourself while others will require that you hire some help. Unless time and resources are things you have in abundance, it would be smart to do all of the necessary research before building the prototype. Very rarely will you be satisfied with the first attempt but having a good place to start will make the process easier going forward.

Location: Once you have a working prototype, you have to decide whether you want it to be made domestically or overseas. For this example, I will assume that you live in the United States. Some products are only made in the United States so there is no decision to make in those instances. For others, you must consider the benefits and costs.

Manufacturing your product in the United States means that lead times, the time between the beginning and end of the production process, will be relatively short for any location in the country. Additionally, the quality of your product will be easier to maintain and improve. You can also advertise that your products are made in the United States which a lot of consumers will be happy to know.

Outsourcing your production overseas means a drop-in quality control, but at a much better price. A plastic product can be manufactured in China for less than half the price quoted by an American manufacturer. However, lead times will be much higher. You could pay significantly more for express shipping but then that defeats the purpose of doing business overseas.

As a general rule, manufacture your product domestically if you want hundreds of copies and in foreign countries if you want thousands. Look into having a representative from your country manage production overseas. The cost of hiring that person is worth preventing the possibility that you receive five thousand devices that are all dysfunctional.

Quoting the product: So you have a prototype and you know where you want to have it produced. Now it is time to shop around. Send your sample to the factory that you want to work with and get an estimate for how much this work is going to cost you. Make sure when comparing quotes from different factories that the quotes are identical. The same quantities, the same materials, the same custom fees. Everything included in one must also be included in the other. If not then you will have to comb through the quote with excess costs to get an accurate price comparison.

Quotes will include terms like FOB which means 'freight on board'. The letters FOB will be followed by a destination so you might see 'FOB New York'. That number will be the price quoted to you is for the goods to be delivered to a port in New York. If you see 'FOB China' then that means the price includes delivery to a port in China. To get those goods delivered to the United States you would then need the services of a customs broker and a freight forwarder.

Customs brokers are the middle-men who are licensed to clear goods through customs. There are also customs agents who are individuals who do the same job. Freight forwarders assemble, collect, and consolidate shipping and distribution of loads that are less than a full trailer. Talking to people in these firms will help you better understand what they do.

Creating your own products: Depending on the types of products you will be selling, you may be able to forgo any type of more traditional manufacturing scenario and instead simply create everything you are going to sell by yourself. There are three different types of manufacturing that you can consider, the first is known as made to stock, which is where you crate the products beforehand and then use your Shopify page as a type of digital showroom.

To ensure you don't overspend on supplies in this scenario it is important to have a clear idea of what the expected demand for your product is going to be. Producing more of a product than you need tends to promote a sale mentality which can severely affect your bottom line depending on the amount of overestimation that occurred. Alternatively, you do not want to underestimate the demand that your product might receive as having too little stock on hand if your shop becomes popular early on can severely curtail your earnings potential in both the short or long term.

Another type of manufacturing strategy is to advertise the fact that your products are made to order based on customer specifications. This type of manufacturing ensures a natural inventory control mechanism and ensure you do not need to worry too much about the demand in the short term, as long as there is a steady stream of work coming in. Unfortunately, this type of manufacturing strategy won't work for every product category as the level of personalization possible will not equal out to the amount of extra time the order is going to take to create. If you hope to make this type of manufacturing work for you, you will need to ensure the added time comes with an appropriate amount of added value.

When it comes to creating your own items successfully, your goal at every turn should be to minimize as much risk as possible. If you have too much of a supply your demand will drop and if you don't supply enough then you might not be able to recoup your costs. As such, the most important thing to do is come up with a realistic business plan and stick to it no matter what.

CHAPTER 4
MISTAKES TO AVOID

*N*ot creating expandable brands and product lines from the start: If you are planning to build a sustainable business brand, you will want a larger umbrella of products to expand your business in the long run. Pick primary products that have plenty of complimentary purchases or can be bundled together with other items. This way you can keep adding items to create a longer product line under your brand. For example, if you zero in on the electronic gadgets niche, you may have a whole bunch of accessories and replaceable parts to sell to under a single business brand.

Go with bundled products and multi-packs if you are looking to score really big with Amazon FBA. Single items that sell are unlikely to be competition free or low competition on Amazon. Almost all products that sell reasonably well have tons of merchants in the category. Also, profit on one item products is swallowed by Amazon fees. Unless you can find a sweet spot between a high-priced product that is also in demand and has low competition, you may not be able to achieve stellar results with single items.

Also, your woes will increase if Amazon sells the product. Unless you have a terrific edge, it is going to be hard to compete with Amazon. Bundling up products or creating multi-packs may require greater time or money. You need to source a variety of items and bundle them. However, it can be highly beneficial for long term profits.

Underestimating the holidays: As long as you are comfortable holding on to these items for roughly 10 months, the deals you can find on decorations during the days immediately after most major holidays can practically guarantee acceptable profit margins on nearly everything you can imagine. What's more, by waiting 10 months before sending them to Amazon, you minimize your storage costs while at the same time taking advantage of all the people who like to plan for the holidays early. Alternately, you can wait until just a few weeks prior to the holiday to post your products and raise the prices even more to grab customers who waited until the last second and as a result, don't care about the costs.

Not considering the demand up front: While selling niche items is a good choice, that doesn't mean every item is automatically going to be a winner. Once you have an idea of the general types of items you want to sell the next step is to assess the relative demand for each of the potential items in question. As long as the items you are thinking about selling aren't extremely obscure, this process should be relatively straightforward. A good way to start researching the popularity of a specific item is to simply type it into the Google search bar and see what options appear under the autofill option. Again, what you are looking for here is a demand that is not being entirely met, so questions about where to find specific items are a great positive unmet desire indicator.

Another good place to look is in the autocomplete results of search engines on websites like eBay or Etsy, places where people are already going to search for harder to find items. In fact, if you ultimately find that the community for buying and selling related items is particularly robust, you may wish to consider starting a store on one of these platforms yourself.

Not listing products the right way: Even though we are told time and time again not to judge a book by its cover, shopping on Amazon, and anywhere online in general, is quite the opposite. One of the vital aspects of any listing on Amazon is the title, which informs potential buyers what the product is all about.

- Add keywords to the title to help the product to rank when buyers search
- Incorporate brand name
- Incorporate the name of the product

Add any features that distinguish the item
- Its use
- Color
- Size

For instance, if you are selling a pacifier, an ideal title would look something similar to this: Deluxe Silicone Baby Pacifier – Easy for Parents – BPA Free – Set of 2 Pacifiers – Blue

Goals for an Amazon product title should do the following:

- Educate potential consumers about the product, even before they read the product page
- Add a few keywords to showcase the product and its use

Not taking full advantage of images: Another important aspect of the product details of items on Amazon is the images included in the listing. They can cause shoppers to click on your listing just because of the quality of the image. That's why you should spend a good amount of time to research images that are top-notch. Amazon product images should include:

- Showcase product size by having a human hold it
- Information images like charts
- Images that include features of the product and compare it to other similar items
- Images of your product being utilized
- The back label
- The item from all different angles

A great resource to find top-notch Amazon images for your listings that are also affordable is AMZDream.com.

Not using enough bullet points: If potential buyers fail to be swooned by your choice of title and images, bullet points are the next best thing to get a straightforward reaction. You have five spaces to include bullet points, but this doesn't mean you only have to use five words or even sentences. I personally use short paragraphs in each of those bullet points to home in on benefits and features of the item. Address common questions and objections as well. Use the first three points to showcase your products most pertinent features and use the other bullet points to answer common inquiries or customer objections.

Not pricing products properly: Opt to sell private label products that are priced above $10. Amazon lists items priced below $10 as "Add On Items, which means buyers cannot purchase your item by itself. They have to make additional purchases to be able to buy your product. Additionally, profit margins for products priced below $10 after deducting Amazon's fee can be rather low for building a lucrative, long-term business. You will need a very higher sales volume to witness recent returns. Ideally, pick products that sell in the range of $10-$30 for higher profit margins.

Few things will kill you like low cost products on Amazon unless you predict an unrealistically high sales volume. You may think inexpensive items carry less risk or are more frequently picked up by customers on impulse. However, selling products for below $5 is not likely to be profitable even with a high sales volume or next to nothing sourcing price. The shipping cost (to Amazon's warehouse) and fees will leave you with a few pennies.

Not treating it like a business: While Amazon FBA is not the same as having your traditional website up and running where you sell products to people, you should still treat the time that you spend on Amazon FBA the same that you would like an e-commerce business. Even though using Amazon FBA allows you to move away from creating your website, this does not mean that you should not take Amazon FBA seriously. You can lose money through this platform if you're not accurate in your estimates or you're sloppy with your profit margin calculations.

Not doing enough research: Another tip that many Amazon FBA users miss is that they don't do research on the Amazon site itself before deciding which products they're going to sell. Even if you enjoy fishing, this does not necessarily mean that selling fishing poles on Amazon is a decision that is going to lead to profits. Look at what's selling the most frequently on Amazon, and take note of any markets that may look like they're being underrepresented.

Having too many similar products: Unlike the notion of a niche website that we've already discussed, you do not have to worry about keeping a product line that is similar when you're using Amazon FBA. Because your seller profile is not going to define the type of business that you're running, you have the freedom to pick and choose the products that you want to sell. This can be great for someone who is good at doing research on products within Amazon's website. By figuring out the profit margin that's possible from certain products that are on the market, you should be able to make better financial decisions for yourself and your business.

CHAPTER 5
TIPS FOR SUCCESS

Free inventory from your house: In my house, and likely yours as well, there are those items that you have not been used, ever! Not since you bought it because it was on sale, or there was a discount on the commodity. You could have used it once and return to the furthest corner of your closet or kitchen cabinet; no matter the case, these items can be turned into cash or better, profit! All you have to do is ship them to Amazon for that to happen.

Go hunting! Look through your book shelves, not all books in your library you like them, get them out and create space for the series you have been dying to read in your house and also reduce clutter. Go into your cabinets in your kitchen, your kids (if you have any) rooms with their permission, of course, your room as well and get rid of anything that you do not use at all. Some items you can get will surprise you; as these items can be used to create profits on Amazon.

Take the initiative and involve your family, friends, and neighbor-if they are willing to do so-and use all these items to earn cash! It can be an excellent way to spend a weekend, go through your trash to make money.

Using dunnage for shipments: The stuff, either puffy or protective wrapper, which you use to wrap your load to protect them from touching the sides of your shipping box that is the definition of dunnage.

There are various things you can use to protect your items so that they can arrive safely to your customer without breakage. The commodities in the list below are things you are most likely going to have in your house already. You can use:

- A newspaper blanket
- A variety of small cardboard boxes for glass items
- From your online arbitrage purchases, you can use the air pillows in them
- Tie printed papers in your everyday plastic grocery bags. This is to protect your shipment from getting in contact with the newsprint.

Free boxes from grocery stores for shipment: At the beginning of your Amazon FBA business, there won't be the need for you to pay for delivery boxes as you might not have the cash for it or you want to save the money you have for something else. You can get shipping boxes for free from grocery stores, your neighbors who have moved recently, or your friends or colleagues that have moved as well as places that recycle their old boxes. This will save you tons of cash. Make sure you select the best boxes out of all those that are at your disposal.

From the grocery store, ask the employees or attendees when they are restocking their shelves if you can have some of the boxes they are using. They are likely to let you come and collect to your heart's content or even when they are restocking come and get the boxes from their aisles.

_____

Lighter fluid to remove price stickers: When reusing shipment boxes, there is the likelihood of price stickers being on them. Removing them is one struggle you will have to endure if you are trying to save money, but getting rid of the sticker residue is another struggle all on its own. When it comes to dealing with the residue from price stickers lighter fluid will do the trick every time.

Be careful when handling the liquid, and this will guarantee the removal of the residue. The process is quite simple, and all you will require is a Scotty peeler to remove the labels. You can use a Ronsonol lighter fluid. To do this, you will:

- Pour some of the lighter fluid on the sticker residue you want to get rid off
- Wait for a few minutes, approximately 5 minutes before you can try and remove the labels
- Using your Scotty peeler, gently try and pry the tag off.

_____

Free inventory from Freecycle.org: Join a group of your area on Freecycle Network to be able to see what people are getting rid of or giving away for free that you can use for your shipments. You might be shocked by the number of things that you can source using this network. I got board games- both used and new-; books, in boxes; kitchen appliances, among other things.

The way it works is:
- Claim an item on the Freecycle Network
- The owner will leave it on the front porch or sidewalk
- Go and collect your item!

And that's it! Fairly easy and straightforward. This makes it easy for you to coordinate with the owner as you will get to set a time that you will pass by to collect it.

Boxes from arbitrage purchases: To be honest, most of the sourcing that you do for this type of business is through online sourcing. This means that there will be shipments sent to you in boxes. Thus you can use these same boxes for your shipments to Amazon. But you have to go to be careful and remove all bar codes. This can be removed or covered up before you can use the UPS label or Amazon.

Productivity tools: There are times when you just need to have a nap without worrying over unnecessarily about the way your online store is doing or how the shipments are fairing or remember if you sent a reply to your customer's comment. Below are some productivity tools that can help you shave off some of that time:

- IFTTT (If This Then That): This is mainly used by sellers on Amazon or eBay. The app is used to alert the sellers of when sales have been made, or stock has been added back into inventory, or it has been added elsewhere.

- Facebook News Eradicator: With various sellers mainly spending their time on this social media platform going through the different FBA groups, it can take much of your time without you realizing it. To help you with this, this eradicator cuts down your extension extremely low. It allows you not to spend so much time on the internet getting to know what all your sources on Amazon FBA are talking about or all seller community groups.

- Cleer Pro: is an online app for online arbitrage. It is a software that makes it easier for you as a vendor to browse easily when trying to look for deals, items or doing your research on Amazon.com

- Gmail Canned Responses: typing a similar response over and over again can get exhausting, and no one wants that kind of stress. Therefore, this app allows you to formulate a response that is going to reply automatically to the type of replies that come from your customers. The same app can be used to respond to an email you get in your Amazon seller inbox. Since Amazon allows you to use your email to respond to customers instead of creating a particular kind of email address, you can use this app.

- Flashback Express: it can only be used on Windows, unfortunately. It can be used to quickly capture and annotate your voice and then upload the video on your screen. This can be used to communicate something that is in your store. Or deliver something that is on your screen to a colleague or your occasional customer. This makes the message more personal than ever, and it can be the best way to explain something to your customers in an easier manner, and it can make you quite popular among other clients. It can bring you more customers as well.

- Unroll.me: There are dozens upon dozens of emails that you receive from a seller on a daily basis about different offers that you are going to get from Amazon. The difference between having this app and not having it, is you are required to need to keep clicking delete or unsubscribe manually. This app allows you to unsubscribe from those emails or offers that you do not want to have in bulk. There are tutorials online that you can use to help you navigate through the app with ease.

Time saving hacks: To save your time as a salesperson when screening your items and scanning them, you can use the $0.00 buy cost to help you when browsing for items mainly in the app's field "Buy$." The time that you spend typing at the expense of the item is deducted since it costs nothing! You can use a calculator to subtract the actual buying price of the item from the profit price and decide on whether you will purchase the item or you will forgo it.

At times, it is not necessary for you to do the math of whether you will get to buy the product; all you have got to do is check if the price you are buying the item is higher or lower than the price of the profit you are bound to make.

An example would be if the cost of the head gear is at $12.99 and the profit you are required to make is at $9.99; you will not buy the item since it costs more than what you are going to get from the profit.

Other ways of reducing the scanning process are through downloading the Amazon 1Button app. It is an extension from chrome that shows you the price of the item you require, and it does the searching or looking or scanning for you.
An instance would be when looking for game boards; the app will let you know if the game is sold on Amazon and the price of the game. This saves you the trouble of going through Amazon trying to find the game and if it is even available and the price as well.

Keep in mind that not always does the search engine provide the results that you are looking for and at times the items might not even be available or found.

Make sure you invest in the best supplies you possibly can get your hands on. There are the common denominators of supplies that most Amazon sellers have in their arsenal and use them. Most of them swear by these items and can attest to their immense help when carrying out their daily sales.

Have a business credit card and checking account: in your daily life, you have a personal credit card that you use mainly to buy your items and spend it as you wish. You also, most definitely (if not, get one ASAP!) keep track of your expenses and savings as well.

You can have a software tracking app on your every expense charged to your credit card, be it personal or business. For the Amazon FBA, you need to have a business credit card and checking account to keep track of what you are spending on and where your money goes. This card and account need to be different from your credit and checking account.

You can use Quickbooks as a way to keep track of your personal and business accounts and credit cards. The app allows you to:

- Keep track of what you have spent
- Know how much you owe your credit card and
- Where you shop at

Run your business like a business: With this being your business, even if you are running it at your house, you need to run it like one. To make shipping easier, create your shipping and prepping station.

It doesn't have to be anything fancy or too elaborate, get a small table and lean it against a wall. Have drawers (they could be colored or whatever pattern you prefer) close by that house all your poly bags, shipping tapes, scissors, liquid fluid and any other necessary appliance that you need to wrap your shipping items and put them in your box.

Having or creating order in your house can help you run your business very smoothly. The station will help you reduce the time spent running around looking for scissors, the shipping tape or trying to figure out where to lay your merchandise at so that you can work.

The area around your working station can function as your prepping station, where you gather all your necessary items, put them together before you move to your working station to put the final touches on your product before shipping them off to your customer.

The station can act as a studio of some sort. When you have laid out your items on the table, you can take a picture of the items and use them for your store on Amazon. The pictures can be edited; changing the color in the background to pure white t put it on the product listing images section of your site. You can learn more on how on Photoshop Elements on this site http://www.secondhalfdreams.com/4202/how-to-create-an-image-that-meets-amazons-requirements/

Know a good deal when you see one: While finding a niche is important to the long-term strength of your FBA store, the most important rule of FBA is that if you can make a profit on it then you should sell it. As such, regardless of what the product is if you find yourself staring at a sale that is 75 percent off or more then there is always going to be room enough there for you to make a profit on the item. The key to not putting too much work into this type of passive income is to always passively be on the lookout for good deals and be ready and able to jump on them when you see them because the best deals are never going to stick around for very long.

Care about your seller rating: Just because you letting Amazon do most of the heavy lifting doesn't

mean that you can let your store run on autopilot. Specifically, you are going to want to be aware of your seller rating and do everything you can to keep it as high as possible. If you sell faulty merchandise or items that fall apart quickly then this number will drop rapidly which means you will want to consider all the costs of a particular product, not just what you pay to take direct ownership of the product. What's more, if you make a habit of selling unreliable items then Amazon can drop you from the service for hurting their image, something that you will obviously want to avoid at all costs.

Consider each purchase carefully: The best online retail arbitrage products are those that are heavily discounted, irrespective of the type of product in question. As a general rule, if you find anything, literally anything that is marked down 75 percent from its original price, then you can likely find a way to sell it for a profit online; whether it is worth it is another question. Another great choice are items that you can purchase in bulk cheaply now, before waiting for natural scarcity to set in six months or so down the line when your investment will pay off in spades.

A great example of this are toys you can purchase from a dollar store that are based on properties that are never going to go out of style such as Disney properties like Princesses, Star Wars or Marvel superheroes. Many of these products are only ever sold at dollar stores which means that after the initial stock dries up there will be thousands of parents out there looking for character specific merchandise that their child has not consumed yet. If you aren't interested in waiting, you can instead group a number of themed items together, knock a fraction of the total profit off and sell the total as a true bargain.

For example, if you purchase five Disney Princess puzzles for a total of $5, knowing that each typically sells for $5 on Amazon, then you can sell all five for $20, still have the group seen as the value, and even make more than a 50 percent profit on the transaction. If you pursue this course of action, you are going to generate a unique UPC code for the group of products, though you can use the same UPC code for multiple groups if applicable.

Don't forget about social media: The most essential social media for any company or brand to have is Facebook. Pretty much everybody uses Facebook, and having an active Facebook page is absolutely essential.

Do whatever you can in order to build your Facebook fan base. Your posts aren't always going to get a ton of traction, but any traction and any traffic matters... plus, if you make a really good post, you're going to see a lot of traffic come from it naturally. That's just how it works with social media.

You're also going to want to consider getting Twitter and Instagram. These aren't quite as popular as Facebook and are more geared towards people in the 16 to 30 crowd, so if your niche aims at people who are older, then you may not have as much success on these. However, having a popular following on these networks can make a lot of difference for you as a company if you follow through with it appropriately and make a lot of posts.

Finally, you're going to want to set up a Snapchat. Snapchat is potentially one of the best marketing platforms because unlike other forms of social media, where only a portion of your followers can see your content without specifically going to your page, a story on Snapchat is visible to all of your followers. If you have a particularly visually appealing niche, Snapchat can be a great way to show people what you're up to and what's up next on your blog. This extra traffic and these return users will, in turn, lead to a big return on your affiliate marketing products.

CHAPTER 6
SETTLE IN FOR THE LONG-TERM

After learning the basics of shipping and making a few sales, there are some things need to be taken into consideration as they are essential to ensuring your business will remain successful for years to come. The traction of your business refers to the progress that your firm, especially a start-up business and the progress it is making as it grows; is the speed slow or fast or is the pace at which it develops as expected?

It is often difficult to get your business to kick off running and selling which in turn bring you profits and raises the cash you require to either repay debts and clear with the bank or start finding new ways of improving the business. The resources that are needed to get your business up and running might not be available, or you are short a few coins, but your reputation might be at stake if you do not keep above the curve of the business and the competition as well.

Understand your audience: As long as you are fully aware of your product and theoretically who may be ready to buy it, then you are already well on your way to understanding your audience. Likewise, sending out customer surveys is a great way to get the basics of the demographics that you are looking for. Once you have a general outline that represents your customer base the next step is to go deep and determine who their social media influencers are. These can be either YouTube or other social media personalities who are extremely popular in certain demographics.

Once you understand who these people are, you will want to consume a fair bit of their content to get an idea of the types of references they make and the types of slang they use. If you want your customers to connect with your brand you are going to want them to feel like they are embracing one of their own. Once you have appropriated the appropriate culture, the next step is to send your products directly to these influencers in hopes that they will like what you have sent and then ideally use or talk about it at some point down the line. While this might initially seem expensive, this should be considered a marketing expense and its results can be extremely lucrative.

It is important to not leave Instagram influencers out of the equation either as recent studies indicate that items that were positively rated by top influencers were directly correlated to an increase of sales of nearly 30 percent, what's more, nearly all of those customers were new to the site which means this type of exposure can be extremely influential. When it comes to creating a buzz around your brand, this type of marketing will give your store a grass roots feel that is extremely popular among the demographics that are the most likely to use the internet to buy goods and services on a regular basis. To find more information on popular influences, Websta.com can provide lists of the most commonly searched for usernames for Instagram and other sites, it also allows you to search hashtags.

Ask for customer feedback: Many FBA sellers underestimate the importance of getting feedback from customers but it is crucial to ensuring your business survives in the long-term. Amazon states that customers are allowed to leave comments on the orders that have been transacted by Amazon, for sellers to view. This is the same for merchant-fulfilled orders.

The FBA orders can work wonders for you as an entrepreneur. The sales can hit the roof and also this can be a way for you to increase your reputation as a seller, even though you are new in the market.

About the customer's feedback, this is a way to conclude a client's experience on a positive note:

- Communication with the seller
- Packaging of the product(s)
- Shipping process
- Customer service
- Dispute resolution- which has to be on point.

Amazon, if not always, helps an average seller to have the best shipping and packaging services that are equal to professional dealers. This is if you are participating in the FBA program.

With FBA orders, the same as any other orders run through or by Amazon; when customers are not satisfied with the product they purchased or with any of the fulfillment services that are provided by Amazon, the feedback received, Amazon will strike through.

If anything does go wrong, there is a chance that the problem mainly isn't with you but with Amazon. The FBA solicitation process value increases so does the tracking changes that your feedback score provides.

You have the option of tracking your comments manually. You need to do this as often as you possibly can. To do this; bookmark the Amazon Feedback Manager section in your Seller Central dashboards. Ratings daily may vary considerably all dependent on the volume of your orders. The more orders you get, the number of ratings will increase as well. It could get to the point of you going through new feedback for hours in a span of three to four months.

You could also use FeedbackFive that is an automatic way of looking at your feedback. How this works is there will be alerts that will notify you of negative, neutral or new feedback.

You can receive the comment in either mail or text form. This is less stressful for you; since you don't have to spend hours going through your dashboard to see if there is any new feedback.

To clear any disputes with your customer that is your fault, make sure you resolve the issue as fast as you can by taking the necessary steps to do so. After, then and only then can you ask for a removal of the feedback. In case you believe it is Amazon's fault, you can request for them to remove the negative feedback.

SET THE RIGHT GOALS

The SMART system is a way of focusing your time on goals that will create the maximum amount of benefit possible. Goals should always have a timeframe, be relevant, achievable, measurable and specific. Regardless of what you are trying to achieve, applying the SMART test is a good way to make sure you are getting the most out of any effort you put in.

_____

Specific: It is important to always have a specific, clear goal in mind whenever you set out to accomplish something new. The foggier the goal, the easier it will be for your mind to come up with excuses to do something more immediately satisfying instead. Having something specific in mind instead gives you something to focus on when your mind starts putting forth excuses. Know your goal and focus on it when times get tough and you will find it easier to power through the right way.

If you aren't sure if your goal is specific enough, run through the 5Ws and H: who, what, where, why, when and how. If your goal is specific enough that you can determine who will be involved, what will be accomplished, where it will be accomplished, why you are doing it, when you will start working on it and how you will see it through then you are likely on the right track.

Measurable: Appropriate goals are those which can be clearly defined between a set of points, one which indicates success and the other which indicates failure. Especially when you are first starting out, it is important to always choose goals that will allow you to clearly know when you are drifting off track. Measuring your progress will ensure that you are able to keep up the good work as you will know that you are hitting required deadlines and meeting all of your due dates with ease.

Attainable: Quality goals are those which are realistically attainable. As previously stated, it is important to always stick with attainable goals, especially at first. In this early state trying and failing, may be worse than not trying at all. This doesn't mean you must always pick goals that are easy, however, easy goals typically lead to fewer rewards. They are fine at first, but eventually, you will want to choose goals that are attainable through additional hard work and planning as they tend to be significantly more rewarding in the long run.

Relevant: Choosing a specific, measurable, attainable goal is meaningless if what you have chosen isn't relevant to your current situation. It is important for the goals you choose, specifically your first few to be as relevant and there fulfilling when they are completed as possible. You are working on building new neural pathways and effort that doesn't directly correlate to reward gives your brain nothing to associate together which makes the entire exercise moot.

Likewise, it is important to pick an initial goal that will easily fit into your current routine. Early goals have few habits to fall back on, add part of them to each day's to-do list and complete it in chunks slowly but surely. Make a habit out of completing part of the task and you will slowly but surely be able to count on yourself to complete more and more complicated scenarios. Like with everything in life, practice makes perfect.

Timely: A goal is not truly a goal unless it has a clearly defined end point. Having a time limit will make it more likely for you to focus on the goal at hand as something that you should work to accomplish right now as opposed to something you are planning on working to accomplish eventually. The timeframe that you choose for success should not be overly ambitious, while at the same time not feeling lax. The point is you should feel pressured to hurry up and get to work, so set a timeframe that you will have to hustle slightly to succeed.

BECOME AN AUTHORITY

In many situations, the word expert and the word authority are often used interchangeably; this is not the case with online marketing, however, as being an authority is everything and being an expert is much worse than simply getting second place. In this case, an expert is someone who knows a lot about a certain niche while an authority is the person that all of the experts agree is the first stop for information on a given niche. To put it another way, authorities aren't authorities because they say they are, they are authorities because when they make declarations in regards to their niche of choice, other people listen.

The benefits of being an authority in relation to a given niche, are much the same as any other authority figure when you speak everyone will listen. This is because those who know you are an authority will expect that you know what you are talking about in any given situation, after all, you must know best. It doesn't take much of an imagination to see how this can directly translate into additional sales when given the proper push. If you can reach the status of authority for your niche you will be able to set the tone for the entire niche as well as have a legion of loyal followers willing to defend everything you say.

When it comes to marketing for your online business or website, it is important to have a healthy social media presence as well as a firm grasp of the importance of SEO if you want to reach out and find new revenue streams. If you also spend time slowly building a reputation as an authority in a given niche, then you will be able to rest easy the revenue streams will come to you instead.

Do your homework: The first step to writing content that will help you to see as though you are an authority in your niche is going to be difficult for some people and easy for others depending on their ability to get online and do the research that being an authority in a chosen niche requires. Put another way, you need to learn enough to know what it is you are talking about in any situation you might find yourself in regarding your niche.

Not to worry, this isn't something that is going to take you years to master as it is perfectly acceptable to focus on a single aspect of your niche to the exclusion of all others. Not only does this have the benefit of ensuring that you will actually get to use the information you are learning at a point in the near future, but it will also allow you to differentiate yourself from any other authorities in the niche without having to actively go head to head with them.

Once you do get to work, it is important to do more than simply becoming familiar with the Wikipedia page on the topic, it means going to the sources that you can find connected to that Wikipedia page and then tracking down there sources as well. You will then want to do this again, and again and again until you can honestly say that you have left no stone unturned. It will unavoidably require lots of hard work and effort, though the results will certainly pay for themselves in the long run.

While you are working your way through this process you may also find it helpful to create a starter guide as if you were writing for someone who is completely unfamiliar with whatever part of your niche you are working at becoming an authority in. While putting together a study guide for a topic that you are not yet terribly familiar with might seem like a poor choice, the fact of the matter is that absorbing the complicated topics you are studying and breaking them down in such a way that anyone can understand will help take the content from something you've learned to something you can easily explain, which is what you will be spending a lot of time doing through your blog.

Limit yourself: When it comes to becoming an authority in something that your niche cares about, it is important to set realistic goals for yourself in order to ensure that you are undertaking a reasonable goal. This means rather than setting out to become an authority on absolutely everything that is going on with your niche, you content yourself to learning everything about a vertical slice of it instead. The more focused your research is, the more breathing room you will have and the easier it will be to get a handle on just what you are taking on. Remember, a jack of all trades is a master of none.

Know your competition: Just as there are going to be major players in your niche that you did research on before committing to a specific goal, it is important to know who your competition is in the authority space surrounding your niche. Finding this person shouldn't be hard, all you need to do is search for your niche on Google and look for the names that come up most frequently. Once this is done, you will then need to decide if you would be better off trying to dethrone them or taking on a subsection of the niche instead. Regardless of how entrenched this other person is, there is always going to be room for another authority in a niche, you may just need to go above and beyond when it comes to determining just where that room actually is.

Create a guide: While it might seem like an odd recommendation for you to write a guide while you are still learning, you will be surprised at how effective of a learning tool it can actually be. Not only will this result in valuable content that can be used in multiple ways later on, but it will also ensure that you are extremely comfortable with the material in general, which will help to get it into your long-term memory as quickly as possible. What's more, you will find that you learn the underlying concepts more fully when you need to rely on the relevant information in its most basic form.

Grow your reach: While it should be easy for your actual customers to think of you as a credible source at this point if you want to truly become an authority figure you are going to need to branch out substantially. Your goal during this phase should be to spread throughout the niche as completely as possible to the point that whenever anyone who is interested in the niche interacts with it, they can't help but see your name. This means you are going to want to spend time on forums talking about the niche and answering the questions that other people might have. Whenever you are able to do so successfully, you can then credit the information to your website, link included.

You will also want to join social media groups for sellers and bloggers in the niche so that you can get to know your competition as well. Not only will this allow you to get an inside look at their strengths and weaknesses, nothing says you are an authority figure like getting a guest spot on someone else's blog. As anyone who runs a blog can tell you, coming up with enough unique content every week to remain relevant can be a serious chore which is why, assuming you have proven yourself to be a reliable source of information in the community, any blogger should be happy to allow you to run a guest blog.

Once you have access to your competition's customers, you are going to want to do your best to take full advantage of the situation. First, you are going to want to ensure that the content you create is cream of the crop, buy a professional post online if you have to, just provide something that people are going to be interested in reading. End the post on a natural stopping point but offer those who are interested in more a follow up on your own site, link included. Finally, seal the deal by providing a coupon code in the post that is good for a serious discount on your own products as well. People will come to your site assuming you are an authority and additional conversions will follow.

Make friends: While utilizing other authorities and experts for what they can do for you will certainly help you to become a more well-known authority in your chosen field, it is important to not let the cutthroat world of online content marketing make you into someone who is only out for themselves. Having a reputation of being a good person, someone that other respected members of the niche community respect is almost as beneficial as being considered an authority. Likewise, you can recommend products and services that you don't even sell which will make everything else that you recommend look sincerer as a result.

This tactic will also lead more of your target audience to feel a stronger connection with you because a basic part of human psychology is that we like people better when they start by putting their worst foot forward.

This is a disarming trait which makes it easier to trust the person in question as it is clear that they really have nothing to hide. As such, your relationship with both the other content creators, as well as your subscribers and your target audience will be strengthened as a result. Finally, your target audience will appreciate the fact that you are committed to telling the truth about a given product or service even when it isn't obviously in your best interest to do so.

Instead of just taking a guest spot on another site, reciprocate, talk about the cool things that other people are writing about or doing and encourage your target audience to broaden their horizons. Not only will this help to strengthen your place in the community and lead to more reciprocation, but it will also show that you are confident enough in what you are doing to not be threatened by other presences in the same space. After all, if you are an authority then you have nothing to fear from those who are simply experts.

Create email blasts: Once you have started gathering a bit of a following, you are going to want to capitalize on that fact by creating a mailing list where you provide even more free content to those who are looking for all of your wisdom that they can get. You can easily utilize the contact form that should already be on your site for this purpose, and even if you aren't ready to start an email blast quite yet, it is important to try and gather as many email addresses as possible for when you ultimately have a use for them.

Email blasts are primarily used as a marketing device, though doing so needs to be handled delicately for the best results. You are going to want to typically stick to a margin that leans heavily towards legitimate content and lightly on advertising if you want your open rates to remain high overtime. As long as you don't overdo it, however, then this can be a great way to get a target audience to trust you to look at things you want them to buy.

You can then use something called an autoresponder to send them new links to products you are promoting automatically once the information has been collected. Consider the following tips to create the type of autoresponder messages that get the response you need to start seeing real results in the long term:

When setting up an autoresponder message, you will want to pick an average of 5 products that do not directly compete with one another but are still clearly related.

In addition to sending out a new unsolicited email every 4 days, you need to track the emails that you do send out and determine how many people opened each email and how many actually bought something because of it. As you gain more information to work off of you can more specifically target your emails to have a better success rate among your target audience.

When it comes to understanding what you can do to ensure that your autoresponder emails are opened, the first thing you will want to do is to send emails from your name directly. Assuming you have connected your name with your brand, opening an email from you should be akin to opening an email from anyone else your readers know. Outside of that, there are several important guidelines to consider to ensure readers keep opening your unsolicited emails for years to come.

35 percent of your subscribers will open any email with the right subject line. This means your subject line should be short and sweet, no more than 10 words but no fewer than 6. The subject line should imply useful content related to the niche in question. This ensures you are at least including something you know your audience should, in theory, be interested in.

When it comes to finding useful content that you know your audience is interested in, the best place to start is with the posts that have gotten the greatest number of views previously and expand on that information. If you expect your subscribers to open content that they know is going to try and sell them something you must deliver on your promise for quality useful content every single time.

Conversions by source: If despite your authority in your niche you find that your conversions by source aren't where you would like them to be, then there are a few things you will want to ensure you are doing properly before moving on to more advanced tactics. The first thing you will want to consider is the HTML email you are using. If it is comprised of one large picture, then if that picture can't be displayed for any reason then you are cutting out a large portion of your customer base. Go back to the testing phase and ensure everything is working in as many different scenarios as possible and see if things improve.

Additionally, your conversions might be down because you are offering up too many choices and your subscribers are experiencing choice paralysis. Especially as your focus has shifted from just an email newsletter to a blog and being seen as an authority in the niche as a whole it is natural for your newsletter to pick up bloat along the way. Slice and dice, shake it up and maybe try something new, your conversions could simply be down because fatigue has set in. You may even want to stop publishing a newsletter for a short period of time, just so people can realize they miss your expertise. Then, when you come back new and improved, your conversion rate should naturally jump as a result.

CONCLUSION

Thanks for making it through to the end of *AMAZON FBA MASTERY COACHING*, let's hope it was informative and able to provide you with all of the tools you need to achieve your goals, whatever it is that they may be. Just because you've finished this book doesn't mean there is nothing left to learn on the topic, and expanding your horizons is the only way to find the mastery you seek.

Now that you have made it to the end of this book, you hopefully have an understanding of how to get started creating your own passive income stream with FBA, as well as a strategy or two, or three, that you are anxious to try for the first time. Before you go ahead and start giving it your all, however, it is important that you have realistic expectations as to the level of success you should expect in the near future.

While it is perfectly true that some people experience serious success right out of the gate, it is an unfortunate fact of life that they are the exception rather than the rule. What this means is that you should expect to experience something of a learning curve, especially when you are first figuring out what works for you. This is perfectly normal, however, and if you persevere you will come out the other side better because of it. Instead of getting your hopes up to an unrealistic degree, you should think of your time spent building your passive income stream as a marathon rather than a sprint which means that slow and steady will win the race every single time.

The next step is to stop reading and to start doing whatever is required of you in order to ensure that yourself and those you care about will be on good financial grounds and stability. If you find that you still need help getting started you will likely have better results by creating a schedule that you hope to follow including personal milestones and practical applications for various parts of the tasks as well as the overall process of acquiring the life changing knowledge and experiences.

In this light, studies show that complex tasks that are broken down into individual pieces, including individual targets, have a much greater chance of being completed when compared to something that has a general need of being completed but no real time table for doing so. Even though it would seem silly, go ahead and set your own deadlines for completion, complete with indicators of success and failure. After you have successfully completed all of your required milestones, you will be glad you took that former step.

Once you have finished the initial process it is important to understand that it is just that, only part of a larger plan of preparation. Your best chances for overall success will come by taking the time to learn as many vital skills as possible. Only by using your prepared status as a springboard to greater profit margins will you be able to truly rest soundly knowing that you are finally taking the right steps into realizing your financial balance and stability, not to mention prosperity.

Finally, if you found this book useful in any way, a review on Amazon is always appreciated!

Jonathan Fitzpatrick

SIGN UP!

Visit our website
www.jonathanfitzpatrickauthor.com
and enter your email address to receive exclusive
bonus contents related to the updates of this book
and find out everything about Jonathan
Fitzpatrick's new publications, launch offers and
other exclusive promotions!

JONATHAN
FITZPATRICK

PASSIVE INCOME

THE HOLY GRAIL OF FINANCIAL FREEDOM

The Side Hustle Blueprint to Learn How to Make
Money Without Being Actively Involved

JONATHAN FITZPATRICK

PASSIVE

INCOME

THE HOLY GRAIL OF FINANCIAL FREEDOM

THE SIDE HUSTLE BLUEPRINT TO LEARN HOW TO MAKE MONEY WITHOUT BEING ACTIVELY INVOLVED

JONATHAN FITZPATRICK

DISCLAIMER

The information contained in this book is for general information and educational purposes only.

This book assumes no responsibility for errors or omissions in the contents on the Service.

This book have no liability for any damage or loss (including, without limitation, financial loss, loss of profits, loss of business or any indirect or consequential loss).

JONATHAN FITZPATRICK

SIGN UP!

Visit our website
www.jonathanfitzpatrickauthor.com
and enter your email address to receive exclusive
bonus contents related to the updates of this book
and find out all about Jonathan Fitzpatrick's new
publications, launch offers and other exclusive
promotions!

JONATHAN
FITZPATRICK

INTRODUCTION

Hi, I am Jonathan Fitzpatrick, a young online entrepreneur. In my first three years of business, I was able to increase my passive income from zero to seven figures by applying different model business.

I started with Amazon FBA and went from zero to six figures annually in my first twelve months of activity. Once I had stabilized, I had integrated a second source of passive income through a business called affiliate marketing. Today I am also a real estate investor, and I earn seven figures a year through these different passive business models.

WHAT IS PASSIVE INCOME OR AS IT IS SOMETIMES KNOWN – RESIDUAL INCOME?

Simply put, it is a receivable you get, even if you are not actively working. It is important to understand that income is different from salary - Income is all that someone receives, whereas, salary is what you get through work, i.e., sale of time.

Passive income means a way to raise resources without the need for the physical presence of the recipient of this income, i.e., money comes in regardless of what the recipient of this income is doing. It is tied to the idea of putting money to work for you, not the other way around.

Now, if you want to ensure a peaceful future, it is important to start generating passive income because that can bring you more security and stability. Understanding the definition of passive income as creating a system that will generate income without (or with little) work, will help you build a better future. The next step is to try and create a passive income, but what if you have no money? Do not worry, that can be taken care of too. It is not easy, but with determination and enough effort, it is possible (and relatively cheap). Let's take a look at the different (and economical) ways to generate passive income.

SECTION

ONE

LEARNING ONLINE METHODS TO EARN PASSIVE INCOME

CHAPTER 1
AFFILIATE MARKETING

Now that we have defined what passive / residual income is, let's define what an affiliate marketing / program is.

Affiliate Marketing is a type of marketing done by sites that register webmasters or people to advertise their banners or links on their websites or on the internet. The webmasters register for free in the affiliate programs offered by these sites and start to divulge a special link, banner, window or any type of advertisement, originated from its register (usually with a personal code embedded). It is a type of result marketing where the webmaster or affiliate of the site only receives money or premium for clicks, impressions or sales originating from your code.

There are several types of affiliate programs like CPC, CPA and CPM. Each of these types generates a certain type of feedback to the user. CPC, or Cost Per Click, generates a return whenever a person clicks on an affiliate program link. CPA, or Cost-per-Action, generates a return whenever a person buys a product or service within a program. CPM, or Cost Per Thousand, generates a profit for every thousand banners displayed on the affiliate's website.

1 - SITES WITH ADVERTISING BANNERS - GOOGLE ADSENSE

If you have a blog or website, which has Google advertising banners, you can win with every click. Some people create blogs or sites and position them well in the search engines, just to place these banners and make money with Google Adsense.

2- AFFILIATE MARKETING FOR COMPANIES

Another way is to advertise other companies/tools and make money as an affiliate. For example, you use a hosting service that you love, make a post or place a banner with your affiliate link and then, with every person that hires this hosting service, you get a percentage. This way, you can make money with every sale or subscription of the product that comes from your site.

3- AFFILIATE MARKETING WITH CONTENT MARKETING

This is one of my favorites. After all, this is what I do. To understand this, let's say that you make a video or blog post talking about a certain product and leave your affiliate link there. Every day, at least one new person gets to know about your work, and that content keeps being on air for years, generating passive income.

4- CREATING DIGITAL PRODUCTS

When we are talking about generating passive income through the internet, another viable option is to create a digital product that does not need support, such as an e-book where the person buys it to read it and by extension, any other digital product that does not need support to generate income. I gave the e-book example because it is simple to create – it's just like a book, only digital.

5 - MINI SITES

These are sites focused only on a specific subject and are very well-positioned in Google and other search engines. They have a great SEO. Within these sites, you can have e-books for sale, or any other digital product that you have created or own. It's like a direct page talking about just one product. For example, in the above option, we talk about if you create an e-book, then it is possible to create a mini-site and make it available for purchase. Every person who enters Google and search for that subject can find your page (mini site) and buy the product.

6- BUYING A SITE THAT IS ALREADY YIELDING

There are sites that have already been on air, for a certain time. They are already making money with Google Adsense. Now, it is possible to invest in such sites and continue to win. In other words, you pay for this site only once, and then generate passive income, if you want, you can work on this site to include new information, work further on SEO and earn even more.

7- CREATE TEMPLATES OR PHOTOS TO SELL

If you understand the subject, it is possible to assemble templates and make them available on several template-selling websites. And the same thing works with photos; if you like taking pictures, you can make money from that also, providing images of food, travel, among many other subjects.

CHAPTER 2
BLOGGING

When talking about passive income, we have to talk about one of the best and most popular ways of generating the same – Blogging. How to make money with a blog even without having a huge audience (avoid the biggest mistakes made by amateurs). The fact of having a blog without ads always instigated people's curiosity: how can it be possible to make money from a blog without depending on clicks?

Honestly speaking, if you go along with the strategy of making money from blogs through ads, you will come to know that the effectiveness of this type of strategy only decreases year after year. The problem with this monetization model is that you need an absurd amount of ongoing traffic to generate some income. This applies to your website or blog as well as to your YouTube channel.

In addition to losing the power to generate revenue, a blog full of ads hinders the navigation of its readers, resulting in a terrible experience. The obvious question which comes up next is – "Is there another way to make money through a blog?". I'll say – "Yes, of course!"

To let you know how to make money from blogging, we'll go point by point and learn about things which are extremely crucial for this strategy to succeed.

1. WHY INBOUND MARKETING IS BETTER, AND WHY DO WE NEED IT?

If you watch videos on YouTube, you must have been through this unpleasant situation where you're paying attention to the content of the video, and suddenly, without warning, an ad begins streaming in the middle of your video. Irritating, right? In addition to displaying ads at the beginning of the videos, stopping the user in between is, in my opinion, one of the worst ways to get attention.

These advertising pop-ups, so to say, play a disruptive role and may rightly be called as misplaced or overkill ads, among others. That interruption method, the basis of Outbound Marketing or Old Marketing still works, no doubt. However, this aggressive and intrusive strategy has been losing more and more relevance. We're basically so accustomed to seeing ads scattered everywhere that we do not pay attention to them anymore.

Inbound Marketing, on the other hand, does not allow you to buy or interrupt the attention of your audience. Your strategy is based on gaining interest. A clear example of this is when you decide to subscribe to a list of emails. Inbound Marketing presents results far superior to Outbound or Old Marketing, especially in Digital Marketing, being responsible for 90% of the clicks on the web and presenting a low cost in the acquisition of a new client.

2. HOW TO WIN THE TRUST OF YOUR AUDIENCE?

The main point of this is: if you just focus on selling and you do not like what you do, and you're not really worried about your audience, people will notice. And they will not trust you! However, if you can gradually win the trust of your readers through quality articles and tips that help them solve problems, they will put you on a higher level in your "trust meter", and the more opportunities to sell a product / service you will have because they know you are not pushing something., but offering a way to solve a problem, an affliction or lack of knowledge.

3. TRAFFIC – IS IT NECESSARY? IS IT ENOUGH?

I'll be honest: It is necessary. It is not enough. And even so, generating an avalanche of traffic is no easy task. Especially if you are creating your first blog, the beginning can be frustrating. Some take months and months to begin to reap the results of your efforts. Others end up giving up halfway, believing they will not succeed.

But you do not have to have a list of 150,000 registered or reach the threshold of 8 million visits to start understanding how to make money with a blog. Now, other than ads spread across the blog (we have already talked about this), there is one other way to make money through blogs: Ads and posts sponsored by major brands. This also depends on an absurd amount of traffic. They look for people who have significant numbers of followers on social networks and a number of at least 100,000 monthly hits on the blog, depending on the niche.

After all, the more people who access that content, the greater the reach of the brand in relation to the final audience. And the higher your audience, the higher the price you can charge for this type of post.

In addition to the high traffic requirement, by investing only in this monetization model, you will be dependent on the interest of other companies in you and your blog may still displease your audience, so it's not enough.

4. AFFILIATE MARKETING – THE NEXT STEP
As mentioned above, Affiliate Marketing works like this:

You join a product. You place your affiliate link on your website or any other media. A user clicks on your link and falls on the product page being promoted. He buys the product, and you earn a commission for the sale.

Now, this is a good way to make money from blogging that did not involve clicks on Adsense ads. Of course, by betting on Affiliate Marketing as a source of income, you cannot go out selling anything. The effect will be exactly the same as crowding your banner site: your audience will lose confidence in you.

So, follow some basic rules: Indicate only those products that you trust and use, maintain consistency with the niche of your blog, and please state that this is an affiliate link to keep it transparent.

5. SELL YOUR OWN PRODUCTS

In the above approach, there is a lot of work which includes: Market research, search for data sources, a mental map of ideas, content generation, hiring a designer, strategy of dissemination and creation of a sales page. In addition, search for partnerships, interviews, integration between sales page and distribution and marketing of info-product, support to new customers. The gain is much greater when you are the creator of the product. However, the work grows to the same extent.

In my opinion, it's a step that every digital entrepreneur who wants to make money with a blog needs to give in a moment. Not to mention that this is not an exclusive choice. You can merge the two strategies for even better results.

6. EXCLUSIVE CONTENT FOR MEMBERS

Many people like to have access to unique content to feel that they have something that most people do not have. And if you can get a loyal audience, who trusts your work, you would surely find people willing to pay a monthly fee to gain access to a little more of your content.

You can create a member-only content area on your blog by making a recurring monthly payment and offering both articles, videos, and PDF materials.

7. INVISIBLE SELLING THROUGH PERSUASIVE CONTENT

When you start selling over the internet, you will find one of the biggest barriers: resistance to sale. In today's world, people have grown accustomed to getting free content on the internet. And many feel truly offended if they need to pay to get something. So you already must assume that people are not ready to buy while consuming content over the internet.

To be characterized as an invisible sale, your recommendation regarding a particular product or service should sound exactly what it is: a recommendation. You already create a connection with the reader and deliver content of value throughout the article. Then, you make a single call to action at the end of the article.

8. ANTICIPATING YOUR AUDIENCE'S WANTS AND NEEDS

Are you a committed fan of any TV series? If so, I think you're pretty anxious when the next season's release date is coming up. This feeling of dreaming about what we cannot have now is fuelled by the trigger of anticipation. This is extremely powerful because it activates parts of the brain linked to happiness, in addition to leaving your reader eager for the upcoming sale. For this reason, it is so used for any type of release. You can make a series of articles, infographics or videos to generate curiosity in your audience. This is the first part of an internet launch.

9. THE TIME TO SHOW YOURSELF AND YOUR PRODUCT

You've done all the work in anticipation. Now is the time to present your product / service through a sales video. It is at this point that you need to reinforce why you are offering your knowledge to people. As well as the results they should expect with their product. Through a well-defined mission that motivates you to share your experience through a product / service and a strong background story, you will gain more public confidence.

CHAPTER 3
LEAD GENERATION WEBSITE

Generating leads from a blog or website is where the financial return of an advertising campaign occurs. Some of the readers click and buy what we are indicating, others click and register in the advertiser's site or simply by clicking. This reader action, if we have a good lead generation strategy in practice, can be encouraged without you having to ask your readers to do so. In the following paragraphs, we are going to discuss some strategies to increase these conversions and make your campaigns highly profitable.

HOW TO WORK WITH CAMPAIGNS FOCUSED ON LEAD GENERATION?

What perhaps many bloggers and webmasters have not yet realized is that they have unlimited spaces for advertising on their blogs and websites. Few realize that the best way of lead generation is to indicate commissioned products and services that are related to the content of their articles. If they use their articles as a weapon in lead generation, their advertising space is unlimited.

Of course, with this type of indication, one must always be very careful not to indicate products and services that are not of good quality for their readers, as they are using their image for this indication and, over time, they might lose credibility if they do not recommend relevant products and services. Therefore, indicating products and services that are related to the content of your articles, is one of the better ways to take as you will also be complementing the need of your readers.

CHAPTER 4
CONTENT CURATOR

It is risky to say that we are at the height of the information age; after all, technology is evolving so rapidly that the future becomes unpredictable. However, it is not difficult to see that we are increasingly surrounded by information and content, especially with the advent of social media, and it is common to find people with difficulties to manage them.

When an entrepreneur decides to bet on content marketing, basically he will have two options: The creation or replication of information present on the web, a process normally done through social media or email marketing. However, when you choose to perform only the second option, you will soon encounter some difficulties. After all, what content really can be relevant to my audience and to my business? It is precisely to solve this type of question that a content curation becomes necessary.

The process involves segmenting and filtering content for later delivery to the target audience, through sharing on accessible channels. To get an idea, every 60 seconds, 168 million emails are sent worldwide, 600 videos are posted on Youtube, and 1500 texts are posted on blogs. Another point that makes curation even more relevant is the fact that content cannot simply be "thrown" into networks without contextualization. Now, this brings us to the next question -

How to curate content? There is a model for conducting a curation, which is divided into three stages:

1. The research, which consists of monitoring news and articles and identifying the best sources. There are several online tools that help the curator's work - we'll talk about them next! The use of Google alerts and RSS feeds from relevant blogs can also be extremely useful to keep yourself constantly updated.

2. Contextualization: As already mentioned, it is important to give meaning to what is published, according to the interests of the company and the profile of the target audience. Through social media feedback, it is possible to evaluate what is working.

3. Last, but not least, we go to the sharing phase, and here we must define through which channels it will be realized.

Searching for links, blog articles, and web-based information that seems relevant and useful to your audience seems like a time-consuming process. However, there are several ways to optimize this work, making this task much more automated and with more accurate results for your marketing.

Firstly, use social networks. Yes, your company's social networks can be a way to filter good content and know which topics are relevant to your marketing. The two most relevant platforms for good curation are Facebook and Twitter - and even if your company does not use Twitter, it can benefit from the site's filtering and search tools. The social network is increasingly investing in relevant and current content filtering in their research.

Secondly, use Social Media Marketing Kits and Tools to filter content by relevance. Example, BuzzSumo is a site that helps you analyze and filter relevant content through topic search. It selects the results of each keyword searched through the number of shares and backlinks of each article and news - exactly the factors that will help you decide the social impact on the Web. This is the favorite tool for several major brands and content producers.

Thirdly, calibrate your searches by content through tools like Social Mention, which focus on blogging and microblogging publications - especially Twitter. This tool helps you better calibrate your search by content, offering the best keyword suggestions related to your search, and finding users who may have shared articles and news relevant to your content marketing.

Other useful tools include Pocket, to store discovered content, and Feedly, to find and organize RSS, etc. Now you already know what content curation is, how it can be beneficial to your marketing and the main tools for the curator. But, to be a successful curator, I am mentioning some of the tips which have been found useful by a lot of people.

1. DO NOT TALK TOO MUCH, BUT RATHER TOO LITTLE

One of the most common mistakes when making a Curatorship is to look for topics and topics in excess. This makes your curation very broad, and the information found will never be treated with continuity and depth.

2. KEEP FREQUENCY WITH YOUR CURATORS

There is no point in starting a curation of content if there is no way to keep this curatorial active over time, right? Check out an interesting frequency - daily, weekly, bi-weekly - for content search and always have new and relevant information for your marketing and business at hand.

3. USE ONLY THE TOOLS AND HABITS THAT HELP YOU.

Another quite common misconception - and little pointed - in companies that begin to perform curatorship is an insistence on what does not work for the team. Often, the professional in charge of the marketing industry requires the use of tools or habits that simply are not productive for the team. Therefore, seek together with your co-workers the forms and tools most adaptable to the reality of your work.

The next question which will be popping up in your mind right now would be – "How to Choose the Right Content for My Content Marketing Strategy?"

Start with the sales funnel. What kind of material will help with conversions at each step of the funnel? You can find a lot of good content that will support your sales funnel and for the buying journey. Then, look at the top questions the sales team faces when finalizing a sale. It is common to have doubts throughout the process, and evergreen content is the perfect solution to answer the questions of your business opportunities. Think about the information you need for your strategy and go after them! Keywords are great for these searches since it is through them that visitors will get to your blog.

Now, onto the final step, how to take good advantage of the content (after you've done the curation). It's no use finding quality material if you're going to leave it in some lost folder of your favorites. Good content needs to be shared with the world!

As we have already said, social media is the first option - and one of the most important - but the buck does not stop there. Email marketing campaigns and newsletters are also excellent vectors for this content, especially if your list is stuffed with quality contacts. And, do not forget LinkedIn. Even though it is a social network, it has a slightly different approach to others. You can create posts in there, and share in groups related to your area of expertise.

Lastly, remember the credit! In content marketing, if you have one thing that is very important is credit! A large part of replicating relevant content is giving credit to the original author by linking to the article and showing to the reader where it was originally posted.

CHAPTER 5
PRICE COMPARISON WEBSITE

This is one of the ways which became popular along with the advent of various e-commerce portals online. Now, the question which stands tall here is - How to enter your virtual store on this channel? Let's say that you already have a good store, offer good products and can reach a good customer base. Your profit comes in every month, but you're still not happy. On the contrary, you want to show everyone that you have a good, efficient, low-priced store and that within your niche, it can present itself as the best option in the market. Well, a good way for you to make it happen is to be able to enter your e-commerce within the price comparison site.

There's more than one way to get your merchandise to come to appear on the internet. One of the most desired by those who bet on the cost-benefit of the products they sell is the insertion of their website into price comparators.

WHAT MAKES THE PRICES COMPARATOR SITES?

If you buy from the internet with some frequency, I'm sure you would've already learned how to search on price comparators. That is, you get the product you want to score, with all your main technical specifications and you play on the internet.

Price comparison sites will assign within a series of websites which offer the lowest prices found. This is an efficient way to carry out screening. With this tool, the user quickly identifies which are the best buying options for that product. Examples include sites such as Shopbot, Buscapé, Shopping Uol, Bondfaro or Google Shopping.

These systems work as a kind of product disclosures and compare the prices among several different electronic trades. The main advantage of them is obvious: they aggregate countless visitors who wish to buy a particular commodity. That way, you buy a package on a price comparator website already knowing with complete certainty the qualification it will give the visitor.

PAGES FOR COMPARED PRICE SITES ARE A GOOD MARKETING OPTION

These pages that compare product prices are nothing more than a marketing option, which, although practical, play a very important role so that you do not give up on a strategy and make sure you constantly monitor your products to make sure your proposal has worked. To do this, you must always analyze the number of clicks and also, always, calculate the rate of return on investment (ROI).

Only then will the shopkeeper be able to know exactly what is the next decision that will need to be made to establish themselves in the market. Another important point to note is the need for price comparison, websites will not be held responsible, in any kind of hypothesis, for the content of the advertisement in question. Thus, it is essential that you convey, through the description of the products and the photos as the product really is, giving the buyer a sense of security and credibility.

YOUR SITE NEEDS TO HAVE A WELL RESOLVED LAYOUT

If you want to reach a wider range of customers, then keeping in mind the fact that the vast majority of price comparators only work effectively with those tenants who own a website, you need to have a beautiful, practical and functional page. If your site is confusing, slow and poorly structured, it is almost certain that the customer will give up the purchase or not feel safe enough to make the purchase through this channel. As has been emphasized before, one of the essential points for your business to progress is that you can convey a credibility of security and trust to the customer.

INVEST IN SECURITY

To emphasize the above topic, you need to obtain security certificates, such as SSL for HTTPs or certifications such as e-Bit. You need to keep in mind that no shopper will think of buying at a store if it goes through your mind that he may have problems putting his personal information in that store to buy a product.

KNOW THE RULES AND PROHIBITIONS OF THE PLATFORMS

In order for your site to work in price comparators, you need to know all the prohibitions and rules of the platforms. For example, you cannot put photos that do not fit reality, and you cannot redirect the client to a site that was not previously informed. These platforms understand this type of situation as characteristics of those who seek to cause fraud and harm customers. So if you do this, you may end up being barred from putting your goods on that kind of platform that compares prices.

CHAPTER 6
DIGITAL BUSINESS INVESTOR
(INVESTING IN ESTABLISHMENT ONLINE BUSINESS)

The internet is very democratic, and for this reason, it is possible to create online businesses of the most varied types, of the most varied purposes and aimed at the most varied public. There is room for all kinds of ideas, with a good deal of willpower and preparation, a person will be able to set up their business online without having to spend a lot of money. Little Investment and Absurd Results! But what do you need to succeed?

Simply put, Strategy Is Everything You Need!

The great secret of those who already know how to make money online is simply to bet all their main chips in a good strategy since the strategy is everything within the digital entrepreneurship. Knowing the best strategies of digital marketing and knowing exactly the right time to apply each one of them can be the most determining factor for your digital business to grow.

With much will and study, you can learn how to make money online in a short time, and you can create a digital business that is profitable and able to bring you all the return you want. So believe me when I say that anyone can become a digital entrepreneur. Anyone can get this done and make lots of money on the internet without leaving home.

To start with, let me tell you about some tips and ways in which you can make money by investing in digital businesses. (Of course, you'll need to invest in knowledge and follow the best strategy pertaining to particular channels). Some of these have already been mentioned and discussed in detail in the earlier chapters of this book.

1. MAKE MONEY WITH BLOGS

The recipe for making money from blogs is simple: Create quality content related to the products or services you want to promote and place sales on "autopilot" using the affiliate programs. As emphasized earlier, there are some cautions when setting up a professional blog:

First, define the niche market that will work, preferably some subject that understands and dominates. It's not a rule, but it helps a lot. Then you can create the blog, write articles related to the subject that will be addressed and finally monetize your project by indicating and recommending the products through affiliate links. Lastly, you need to create your audience, generate massive traffic on your blog, or you risk writing and no one reading, which in addition to being frustrating, will not bring profits.

2. EARN MONEY WITH GOOGLE ADSENSE

Here is already another strand of digital marketing using blogs to monetize your projects. The creation of the blog is very similar to the one mentioned in our first tip, but in this case, you will not indicate any product. Briefly, blogging about making money using Google Adsense, needs many articles and strategic spaces on the site so that the ads appear on the screen of your readers, and they click easily. You will win per click. However, you need to be cautious that you don't overkill it, as has been warned before. If you ask me personally, I would say I prefer the first option over this one.

Some other things which you can keep in mind while investing in this:

a. Articles have to be well written using on-page SEO techniques and need to be large, at least 500 words.

b. Not all niches work with Google Adsense, choose niches that have many visits.

c. Create lots of articles and do heavy SEO work because this type of monetized site only yields profits if you have a lot of organic traffic.

d. Always optimize your projects by choosing the correct places to place the ads and tracking the click metrics.

3. HOW TO MAKE MONEY ON FACEBOOK

Here we already enter a world half parallel to blogs. Social Networks, especially Facebook, can be a good place to look at how to make money on the Internet. The fastest way to make money on Facebook is by advertising on Facebook Ads, in which case you will need to invest in generating traffic on your affiliate links.

Briefly create publications on your timeline or on fan pages indicating a product or service for people to buy and all distribution of this content is made through Facebook through sponsored ads.

4. GENERATE INCOME WITH SEO

In a nutshell SEO is the set of techniques that aim to position a website in the first places in search engine results, especially Google. You can do this work on your own projects, ranking your sites, generating organic traffic and free. You can also do SEO work professionally by offering this type of service to other people or companies that have an interest in positioning your websites well in the search engines. These SEO techniques go far beyond writing optimized content, in fact the biggest job is the SEO Offpage (Creating External Links).

5. MAKE MONEY ON YOUTUBE

This tip could not be left out, YouTube is now the second largest source of organic traffic on websites and blogs, it has great visibility, and many people prefer watching videos than reading articles. The 3 popular ways (not exhaustive) to make money with Youtube videos:

a. Create videos on miscellaneous topics and monetize on Youtube Adsense.

b. Create daily videos and become a Youtuber, achieving marketing contracts with large companies.

c. Create short videos explaining the characteristics of some product and indicating your affiliate links.

I suggest you choose only one of these ways to make money online and focus on it because at the beginning, too much information can cause confusion and if you do not have focus, you will have problems. Once you get your first profits on the internet, you can expand your digital business and multiply your results. But, do remember – invest in knowledge and follow a tried and tested strategy – only then will you be able to excel in this area.

CHAPTER 7
LOCAL BUSINESS MARKETER
(SOCIAL MEDIA MARKETING)

Many local businesses are unable to visualize themselves in the midst of Inbound Marketing and Content Marketing. The reason? To think that they are methodology incompatible with their realities and that the benefits are clearer for businesses of national scope. However, several local enterprises that started investing in this mindset have had concrete results, proving that the model works. One can use the strategies wisely to deliver results for diverse local businesses.

We have some cases of local companies that used, among the various strategies of Inbound Marketing, the content marketing to aid in this gain of scale – Douglas Lima, Koetz Advocacy Office and many more. The interesting thing, and what you may realize, is that such strategies work for companies from different niches. Photography, advocacy, dentistry and wine trade have already confirmed that it is possible to generate great results with practice. Other segments are possible as well. One just needs to invest money and time wisely.

So, even if the company is a local business that depends on people's on-site visit, making use of content marketing can generate quite impressive results. In addition to being a viable strategy for local SEO, it also serves to nourish an audience by creating a community of loyal customers.

You can use Inbound marketing (specifically in cases of local businesses) to educate the audience and potential customers; be a reference in a certain subject related to your market; and influence the purchase decision.

Check out a few steps you need to take into consideration to start thinking about your content marketing strategy:

1. POSITION YOURSELF!
First of all, you must think about the persona that your company wants to reach, the desired positioning and the type of content that makes the most sense to be published.

Does your client need to learn about the topic? This is often the case in health, wine, law, fashion, among other areas. People have curiosities and doubts about subjects they are interested in, and they like to receive tips on these topics.

Is your work interesting in itself? Often, photos of how the weekend was at a ballad or bar already help generate interest and comments. If it is still none of the above, what is interesting and is around your market? The calendar of events of the city in the week for a taxi co-op? The latest football news for a sports bar? The latest releases of music videos and songs for an alternative ballad?

2. TRY TO CAPTURE THE CONTACT OF THE VISITORS

Create ways to collect the emails of your users. Whether through blogging, landing pages, or contact forms, keep in mind that those users who are entering their email somewhere on your site are potential buyers of your product or service. There are endless ways to convert your visitors into leads. In blog posts you can have a field to subscribe to a newsletter. This can be at the end of the posts or even in the blog sidebar, in a popup or in the page footer.

Another way to capture these contacts is by creating rich materials and making them available for free download on a Landing Page. If you own a mechanic shop, you can create a checklist for the driver to do in the car before a trip. If you are a nutritionist, you can create a healthy eating guide for the summer. If it's a language school, you can create a quiz to test the knowledge of your visitors.

3. INVEST IN ADS TO TARGET THE EXACT AUDIENCE LOCALLY AND HAVE INITIAL TRACTION

It does not mean forgetting to work other techniques like SEO of your blog, for example. But investing in ads will give a traction, at least initially, to your business. Campaigns in Google Adwords or Facebook Ads have an incredible targeting factor, which is crucial for your local business or for your client's business.

4. KEEP ACCOUNTS ACTIVE IN SOCIAL NETWORKS AND PROMOTE YOUR CONTENT

People often look for stores on social media. This usually happens after they already know your business. So create the accounts using the name of your company, or if it is not possible, as close as possible. Social networking for local businesses can be important to do various actions like sweepstakes, contests, put information (menu, courses available, etc.), address and other things. In addition, of course, to be used for you to share the content produced.

Stats of 2019 show that over 40 million small businesses have pages on Facebook. Therefore, being on the largest social network on the planet is no longer a differential, but a basic aspect within Digital Marketing.

5. RELATIONSHIP

With a consolidated audience and leads generated, you need to think about how that relationship will be between your company and your customers. One advantage of using marketing automation is being able to create different streams for different audiences. That is, you can have a flow for sending newsletters and another for sending offers, coupons and promotions.

The important thing at this stage is to follow good email marketing practices to get the most out of it.

6. PLAN THE MEASUREMENT

Measure your actions online with efficiency is one of the biggest advantages of Digital Marketing. But how to measure when sales are offline? This is a fairly frequent question in face-to-face sales ventures, but there are a few existing solutions to clear up this nebulous issue.

As I said earlier too, the possibilities in the field of being a social media marketer (esp. for local businesses) are countless. With patience and good work done, the results should appear organically for your client's company in a few months.

CHAPTER 8
OUTSOURCED ONLINE SERVICE

What do people mean by this? Outsourcing services or Outsourced Online Services is a resource in which a company transfers to a third party, the responsibility in contracting and maintaining the legal relationship maintained with the employees. That is, it is the delegation of certain activities to another legal entity so that it fulfills with the execution of the labor tasks within its business.

Some business owners believe that outsourcing is a complex process and can create serious problems in the execution of internal activities. However, this thinking has changed, and outsourcing is becoming more and more accepted, even at the moment in which the legislation has expanded possibilities in the scope of services that can be contracted in this modality. Why will this attract a number of diverse clients?

COST REDUCTION
The first advantage is the one that attracts the most interest of the entrepreneurs: the reduction of costs. It is known that the labor charges, resulting from the correct application of the country's legislation, significantly affect

companies, often causing a negative impact on the very development of activities.

By outsourcing, the relationship between cost and benefit is positive for the company's financial balance. This is because it involves costs lower than those required for the formation of a team and for the execution of activities within the business organization.

In addition to these issues, it is also worth mentioning that you can become specialized and offer professionals who have the greater technical knowledge, allowing productivity gain and, consequently, financial gain for the company. This is specifically important for those of you who are pretty experienced in one or two fields.

Finally, another indirect reduction of costs concerns the reduction of the structure of the Human Resources Department. This is because outsourcing causes a reduction in the demand for hiring, layoffs and the management of payroll and benefits paid to professionals.

TIME OPTIMIZATION

This is an interesting advantage related to the outsourcing process. This is because outsourcing allows the optimization of the time of managers and the professionals themselves since several operational activities are carried out by the companies that provide the services.

For example, the manager does not need to dedicate part of his time to preliminary interviews with candidates for a particular position, since the outsourced company will carry out the entire hiring process. In this sense, these professionals, as managers and directors, can focus the exercise of their functions in more strategic areas for the business. This allows for better decision making and, consequently, results.

PRIORITIZATION OF INVESTMENTS

The fact that a company elects to contract outsourced activities allows greater prioritization of investments for the organization. This is because outsourcing reduces the need for expenses with training and qualification of professionals since this task becomes a responsibility of the outsourcer.

This gives the company the possibility to prioritize its investments. Thus, you can privilege the use of your resources for strategies that are focused on the growth and development of the business.

SIMPLIFYING THE ADMINISTRATIVE STRUCTURE

This is a fairly obvious advantage when it comes to the benefits of outsourcing. It is natural for the company, when contracting outsourced employees, to guarantee the easy organization and management of cost control, optimizing investments, and avoiding problems related to administrative practices, impasses and even legal issues.

FOCUS ON HIRING EXPERTS

Another interesting benefit that is the Achilles heel of many organizations is the hiring of professional experts, and this is the major part where you as an outsourcer come in.

Outsourcing allows the hiring of more skilled and experienced employees. This circumstance guarantees the improvement in the quality of services and lower risks of hiring professionals who will not work efficiently and productively. This is because outsourcing companies usually invest in training and supplying professionals who stand out in their markets with specific skills and technical know-how.

All these reasons point to the obvious, the much widening gap and ever-increasing demand for outsourcers. One major thing which you need to keep in mind while monetizing this is not to diversify too much too early while entering the space. Quality work done with limited clients will go a long way in establishing your credibility and building a base for exponential growth in the future.

CHAPTER 9
JOB BOARD WITH A TWIST

The job board is the largest career website and gathers open opportunities in more than 3 thousand companies of the most varied segments. The service can bring many benefits to you who are looking for your first stage, or already have experience and need to relocate. If I were asked to list the main benefits of the job board, they would be the ones mentioned below:

1. YOU DO NOT NEED TO PAY ANYTHING

To use the services of you do not need to pay any fee. The registration is and always will be free for the candidates. Therefore, the site will never request your bank or credit card details.

2. YOU DO NOT FIND FALSE VACANCIES

The work is paid by the contracting companies - and never by the candidates. That's why all posts posted on the site are not real. After all, companies pay to make this publication, and it would not make sense for them to pay to advertise a vacant ghost, right?

3. YOU CAN USE THE SERVICE VIA THE APP

You can use the service for free also through the VAGAS app, available for Android and iOS systems. To download, go to the app store on your device and search for the term "VAGAS.com" or "Jobs."

4. YOU CAN SEARCH FOR VACANCIES IN ALL TYPES OF COMPANY

5. YOU CAN REFINE YOUR SEARCH

The search cannot be made from a job title or keyword, for example, "marketing analyst." The first results are presented in order of decreasing date, that is, from the most recent to the oldest. From there you can refine the search by city, country, areas of activity (Marketing, Administration, Communication, Engineering, for example), hierarchical level (junior / trainee, full, senior) and PCD.

6. YOU RECEIVE ALERTS OF VACANCIES IN YOUR E-MAIL

When a vacancy with your profile is published, you receive an alert directly in your e-mail, to register as soon as you can.

7. YOU CAN ACCESS YOUR APPLICATION HISTORY

In your registration, you have access to all your application history made by the site or the app.

8. YOU KNOW WHEN THE COMPANY HAS READ YOUR RESUME

To find out if your resume has been read on some application on the job board, you can check the viewing status in your history. Resumes read are flagged with the green icon "curriculum viewed."

9. YOU DO NOT NEED "IQ" (WHO INDICATES)

To compete for a place published in, you do not need the nomination of anyone. Just meet the ad's prerequisites and apply.

10. YOU CAN FIND DETAILS ABOUT YOUR AREA OF WORK.

It gives you important details about the positions, what you do, how much you earn and even the most frequent training of the people who work in these positions.

CHAPTER 10
CRYPTOCURRENCIES

Cryptocurrencies have come to revolutionize the way of doing business. We live in one of the best times to make money almost anywhere. The cryptocurrencies are one such example and they have come to transform the way of doing business and obviously making money.

On May 5, 2018, a tenth of a thousandth - four decimal places or 0.0001 - of a Bitcoin was worth about US $ 0.97, according to the CoinMarketCap, making now the best time to invest in Bitcoin and the crypto-coins. Learn more about this below.

1. MICROTASKS TO WIN CRYPTOCURRENCIES

This is an option that only requires you to have a computer and some free time. You can do some micro-tasking for someone or some service and win crypto coins in return. These microtasks can be something like downloading new applications for testing, watching videos, doing online surveys, etc. Some services that provide these are: microtasksBituro, Coin Bucks and Bitcoin Rewards

2. BUY & HODL

A safe way to make money online is to buy good crypto coins that have a fundamental use, case and keep them until you get fair market share. For example, crypto-coins like: Bitcoin, Ethereum, Litecoin, Monero and several others.

All of these are safe purchases most of the time. You can buy and hold them for a long term because they are required to appreciate against the fiduciary pairs of USD, EUR, etc.

3. BUY AND HOLD CRYPTO COINS TO GET DIVIDENDS

Another smart way to win through Crypto Coins is to buy and keep Crypto Coins that pay dividends. There are many that give you a fair share just by guarding them and you are not even required to wager on them, especially in a wallet. Some of these crypto-coins are: NEO, COSS, KuCoin and CEFS.

4. STAKING CRYPTOCURRENCIES

This is a great way to win, because you get the double benefit of price appreciation by owning good crypto coins, plus the additional reward of dividends for staking the coins. Staking is basically holding 24×7 crypto coins in a live wallet, thus gaining additional new coins as reward for staking and protecting the blockchain network.

5. MASTERNODES

The execution of masternodes of cryptocurrencies to obtain an intelligent passive income is also a way to win in the world of the cryptocurrencies. A masternode is simply a complete node of cryptocurrency or computer wallet that keeps the complete copy of the blockchain in real time, just as you have full Bitcoin nodes, and are always active to perform certain tasks. To perform such tasks, different networks of cryptomers pay the owners of the masternode.

6. DAY TRADING WITH CRYPTO-COINS

If you understand and are good at technical charts at various intervals of the day, this method of gain is for you. You can exchange different days of crypto coins in various trades. The idea is simple - buy low and sell high when you hit the target. This method works very well for a technical chart person because crypto coins, being a volatile market, can range from 20 to 50% in a day, depending on the choices you make.

7. WORKING FOR CRYPTO COINS

If you are a developer or a tester, a writer or a designer, you can start earning encrypted coins immediately by swapping your services for it. There are numerous platforms and sites that offer Bitcoins in exchange for their service.

8. ACCEPTING CRYPTO COINS IF YOU ARE A TRADER

Another way to make money online with crypto coins is to accept them in exchange for your products or services if you are a merchant. As a merchant, you have access to many Bitcoin crypto-coins and payment processors that can help you to accept them.

Even online business owners and e-commerce sites can adopt this form, thereby obtaining the double benefit of price enhancement of crypto-coins and earning crypto-coins directly.

In addition, in order to be able to mine and earn with crypto-coins, you must have access to cheap electricity to operate the mining equipment along with the technical know-how of how to take care of the software and hardware of the mining material.

CHAPTER 11
APP DEVELOPMENT

There is a lot of money involved in the application trade, billions of dollars. Certain types of applications are responsible for earning much of this money, while others are not able to generate much profit. The list of most profitable apps may be slightly different than you think. This chapter will explain all about how an application makes money and give you some ideas on how your application can become highly profitable.

The mobile market has grown considerably in recent years, and experts in this area expect continued growth. The use of the internet by mobile devices has surpassed the use by desktop in 2019, and more than 80% of Internet users have smartphones. With such impressive numbers, it is no surprise that large companies and investors want to join this world market.

If you are new to this market, you want to get into it or you just have an interesting idea for developing an application, one of the first things you should ask yourself is about the profitability of this investment. Developing an application is a difficult job, and you should want to be rewarded for all your work.

WHICH PLATFORM MAKES MORE MONEY FOR DEVELOPERS?

First and foremost, you need to choose which platform (or platforms) you want to use for the development of your application. This can significantly affect the potential for profit, as there is a difference in market presence and popularity. For this metric, let's evaluate the platforms based on the percentage of application developers earning at least $ 5,000 dollars per month for their applications.

The first place in this category is iOS, Apple's platform, with just over 25% of its developers making more than $ 5,000 a month. Android continues to be a great platform option because of its market presence index. 18% of Android developers earn more than $ 5,000 for their apps monthly. Despite this, it is worth noting that Android has a different form of profitability, since much of the total revenue coming from applications is the responsibility of the platform's top developers. The iOS platform, however, has a slightly more balanced division, increasing the chances of making money on this platform, even being a beginner.

Platforms that are not so favorable to people who want to make a profit from applications include the Blackberry operating system and the Windows mobile platform. The Blackberry does not have a market presence anywhere near iOS or Android, and its owner, RIM, sees its market share and financial gains declining annually. Windows has

Microsoft in its favor, but in the end, it's not as popular with smartphone users.

While niche platforms can generate a certain profit, they should only be considered after your application already generates income on more popular platforms. From the moment your application succeeds, it is more feasible to expand its performance to other platforms.

WHAT KIND OF INCOME DOES AN APP GENERATE?

Apps are great investments, and we cannot deny it. By 2018, global application market revenue reached $ 52 billion. That's around $ 10 billion more than 2017. Many experts predict growth of around 18% by 2020. Gaming applications dominate the list of most profitable applications. Bandai Namco Entertainment's Dragon Ball Z Dokkan Battle game has an estimated $ 2 million daily gain, while King Digital Entertainment's popular Candy Crush earns $ 1.6 million per day through in-app purchases. Supercell, the company behind the Clash of Clans and Clash Royale games, earns more than $ 2.3 billion annually.

HOW MUCH MONEY DO SUBSCRIPTION APPS EARN MONTHLY?
With more than 1 million subscribing users, Match Group's Tinder is a great example of an app that manages to make lots of money through in-house purchases. Tinder's relationship application has a free download but earns money by charging for bonus tools like Unlimited Likes,

which gives users unlimited opportunities to get new combinations. The "plans" added to Tinder allow users to get new combinations from other locations, while boosts allow users to be able to make their profiles appear first to users in a certain area. In 2018, Match Group generated an estimated revenue of $ 285.3 million dollars. This new revenue model from Tinder has made it one of the most profitable applications worldwide.

On a smaller scale, individual applications are also capable of generating significant revenue. The Hooked application from The Telepathic earns around $ 2 million annually and is a relatively simple idea. Users can access suspense stories in the form of messages, through weekly, monthly, and yearly subscriptions. The app creates interest in users through interesting stories but requires a signature so they can figure out the ending.

The Kayla Itsines Swet with Kayla application serves as an example for novice application developers. The app offers 28-minute workouts and a diet. This app quickly gained users, generating something close to $ 45,100 dollars and approximately 9,000 users daily.

WHAT ARE THE NEXT TRENDS FOR APPLICATION DEVELOPMENT?

As you might note, there are several opportunities to get money in the application market. This market has managed to grow significantly since its inception and has no signs of slowing growth. Console applications can be able to generate a considerable income, but there is still plenty of room to grow within less complex and more popular platforms. And, finally, Smart TVs and Smart Watches still need to grow next to the consoles and will probably become part of the final expansion of this market until new devices come out in a concrete way.

CHAPTER 12
KDP

When it comes to publishing your first book on Amazon, it is normal to have butterflies in your stomach. To begin, let's talk about getting started on the book, and we'll take it from there. If you choose to write your own book, make sure you gather as much information about the subject in hand before you get started. It is important for you to gather all relevant information so that you are able to elaborate on every topic in detail and not miss out on anything.

Alternatively, you can choose to hire a writing agency to write a book for you. If you choose a writing agency, always give them all the information that you gathered so that you are both on the same page. This saves you a lot of time by avoiding going back and forth with editing, and it helps you to publish your book a lot faster. Once you have the content of your book covered, you need to decide on the cover for the book. You can get help from designers and freelancers that you can easily find on the Internet. If you prefer not to hand over the responsibility for the cover to someone else, you can always select a cover on the KDP website. Once you have uploaded the manuscript, you will get different options and be given a brief description of the eBook.

If you are looking for affordable services, Fiverr is a good choice. It has awesome covers starting at just $5, and you can get somebody to design a paperback and kindle cover for you at an affordable price. Once you get the cover sorted, tell them to give it to you in a PDF format, as this will help for when you are uploading the book on the Kindle publishing website. Once you have the content of your book sorted out and have a cover, it's time for you to publish your first ever book on Kindle Direct Publishing (KDP).

First, you need to sign up on KDP. Then, you need to select the title and sub-title of your eBook. Once that is done, you need to upload your eBook and the manuscript for the paperback design. The website is self-explanatory, so it's very easy for you just to follow the steps, get to the end, and finally publish your book on Amazon Kindle. It doesn't take a lot of time; in fact, your book could be live in just a few days!

We have spoken about people's preference for eBooks or paperbacks. However, there is a third type of people, the audiobook lovers. Some people prefer listening than reading because it's more convenient. Instead of missing out on this audience, get the help of ack.com, a sister company of Amazon. You don't even have to sign up on this website as you can use the same login details that you use on Amazon. Here, you can add a title for your book, look for it on Amazon and either upload the audio files already narrated by you, or ask them to do it for you. Audiobooks take a while to be produced, but they shouldn't be neglected as you manage to cover a section of people who prefer to listen to books and you leave yourself no room for error.

CHAPTER 13
FULFILLMENT BY AMAZON (FBA)

Another popular method of earning money online is through FBA, which stands for Fulfillment by Amazon. It is an interesting platform that allows business owners to sell products on Amazon using the FBA platform. This platform basically enables buyers to choose products that can be delivered by Amazon. It is a popular method of online marketing because Amazon takes care of the shipping and delivery of a product thereby making it safer to trust. While this may seem extremely convenient for many people, it is one of the most complicated ways to earn money due to the amount of responsibility on your shoulders. Not only do you need to ensure that deliveries go out on time, but you also need to ensure that they are done in a precise manner and that there is no damage to any of the products. You get paid by Amazon depending on the delivery of a product. Also, you need to have your own space to store the product even if it is for a short time, and you are responsible for the packing of the product as well as returns. The pay-out for FBA is not that high, and there are more chances of making money with affiliate marketing.

When it comes to business owners, affiliate marketing is still the number one choice to promote products, for a number of reasons. One of the best things about affiliate marketing is that it is cost effective and as a business owner, you only need to pay for the number of products sold. It also helps create brand awareness in a more effective way.

Although some business owners still believe in advertisements on social media websites and search engines, none of these prove to be as effective as affiliate marketing because of the kind of exposure that the product gets with the publishers. This means that compared to other passive sources of income, affiliate marketing offers higher returns. This is because of the number of opportunities all around you. Affiliate marketing is not a complicated process as compared to the other ways to earn money online, and it happens to be the most convenient way as you do not have to worry about enhancing your skills or figuring out complicated programming or coding.

I started my entrepreneurial career online with Amazon FBA and my life has completely changed in just twelve short months.

More so, you would be envious of the amount of freedom I have to juggle and balance my personal and professional life. When was the last time I did something I love and enjoy? Well, I currently am. I love writing and disseminating knowledge. But if you are speaking in the realms of hobbies, then you should know that I do not miss any of my evening book club sessions. In fact, just yesterday afternoon I managed to attend a painting class, grab a drink with a friend and still managed to be home on time to read my niece a bedtime story. I believe that now I have your undivided attention.

These are the perks that have come with FBA. Fulfillment By Amazon. This is the gold mine that is little understood by those who know about it, let alone less publicized to the general public. For those who are quite familiar with the service, they understand that it is as simple as Buy; Ship; Receive Payment. Then why is it so complicated if it seems as natural.

Well, truth be told, FBA is rather intensive. Regardless of Amazon handling a huge chunk of the program, the bit left to the sellers is not a walk in the park. But I suppose that you already know this, and that is precisely why you are here. You understand what it takes to achieve your financial goals. With your primary goals set out, it will be a far easier job wading through these waters. Add that to an active and fueled mindset and a prosperous story is already being penned.

Fulfillment by Amazon (FBA) is often considered a subset of the dropshipping industry with a few major differences. Whereas with traditional dropshipping a third party is responsible for the sourcing and fulfilment of the orders, merchants in a Fulfilment by Amazon relationship send their items to Amazon who is then responsible for storing and shipping the items in question in return for a portion of the profits from the sale of the item. If you have an item that you are interested in creating a private label for but you weren't sure where the items were going to be stored or how you were going to find time to fill all of your future orders, then FBA is the answer.

In addition to making the physical transaction part of an online sale much less of a hassle, those who participate in the FBA program also get preferential treatment when it comes to search results as well as how their packages are shipped. Amazon power users who take advantage of the Amazon Prime membership option receive free 2-day shipping on countless products that Amazon sells directly, but also, on all of the items sold by those in the FBA program.

This means that by simply signing up for FBA you are already placing your future products at a huge advantage when compared to similar products that you will one day be competing against. The amount you are charging for shipping will also affect your Amazon rating in several ways, but suffice it to say, a lower shipping cost is always better. This, coupled with 2-day shipping, goes a long way towards creating positive mindshare, even if your product costs a little more, or is of a new private label brand that the customer has not yet heard of.

How it works

FBA works by allowing sellers to send their products directly to the nearest Amazon fulfilment facility where the products are then stored until they are sold. You then have the option of paying for additional preparation or labeling services as required while paying a monthly storage fee based on the amount of space your products require. Then, once a customer finds them online, Amazon takes care of all of the fulfilment tasks, including the all-important customer service and returns portion of the process which a more traditional dropshipping service would leave up to you.

It is important to understand just how valuable the fact that Amazon is fulfilling the orders in question is, especially when it comes to private label products from a new company. The Amazon name carries quite a bit of weight with customers, and having that name involved in the transaction will make them much more likely to go ahead and pull the trigger on the transaction in question. While they will hopefully become a loyal follower of your brand someday, being an FBA member gets you in the door. Studies show that FBA sellers typically see as much as a 30 percent boost in sales compared to more traditional sellers.

In return for the perks, FBA members pay a $40 monthly fee as well as a percentage of the sale price of each item. You will also be required to pay fees related to the weight of the item when it comes to shipping, any handling fees, pack or pick fees and storage fees based on the square footage.

Additionally, you will be required to pay fees related to individually labeling all of your products as you will not want them commingled with other similar products as this will only dilute your brand. If you are unsure if this fee structure will fit the private label products, you may be hoping to one day sell you can check out the revenue calculator available on the official FBA site to determine if your idea is likely going to be a success.

When it comes to fleshing out your business plan it is important to factor in the benefits in terms of exposure that you will likely receive as well as any costs you might incur. This is especially true if you are going to be creating your own product line as you are going to need all of the potential customers you can get. If your initial idea does not appear as though it is going to work with FBA, you may want to consider alternative types of products as the solution is out there, you just have to do the work and find it.

A private label brand is any brand that it is not owned by a major company or organization. Over the past 20 years, private label brands have seen nearly double the growth of more mainstream brands, and the growth in niche markets where the importance of individual ingredient lists is much higher; much like customer interest levels when it comes to getting to know the creators of unique brands.

This is in large part due to the greater amount of perceived control that goes along with these types of products and it is something you can use to your advantage if marketed properly. What's more, when you decide to create your own private label you will have complete control over the branding and marketing of the product in question, allowing you to create something truly special that speaks directly to your target audience. Additionally, you will have the added advantage of perceived value as you don't have to deal with all of the added waste that comes from working with a major brand.

THE PRODUCT

For me personally, this is the most difficult part of starting a business. The beginning. The foundation, perhaps. Knowing what to sell to people is like knowing the exact shirt and tie combination to wear for a specific job interview. A polished cover letter and rehearsed answers for the interviewer's questions are far less effective if you dress inappropriately. Too casual is disrespectful and too formal makes you look desperate.

The items you choose to sell to people say something about you. Regardless of whether or not you have any practical use for the product, your signature will be all over them (sometimes literally). The material quality, the packaging, the storage conditions, the handling. While a one-time customer may not notice a lot of those things, a regular customer will likely be looking at all of those things and more.

CHOOSING A PRODUCT: If you did not start your business with a creative idea of your own already in mind then you will need to look for an opportunity. Any of the following is a great place to start

- Opportunities in Keywords

- Building an Interesting Brand

- Identify and Solve a Pain Point

- Identify and Cater to Passions

- Look for an Opportunity Gap

- Utilize Your Own Experience

- Capitalize on Trends

- Opportunities in Keywords

KEYWORDS: Starting from the top, we have opportunities derived from search engine keywords. Keywords are the words and phrases that users type into a search engine. Knowing a little bit about search engine optimization (SEO) is essential if you want to be competitive online. A lot of business owners are willing to handsomely pay savvy individuals to manage their advertising campaigns.

Anyway, the idea here is to find keywords that have a high search volume (a lot of people looking for it) and low competition (few good matches). That right there is a golden opportunity. Giving the people something that they already want means you can launch with a smaller ad campaign than if you were trying to get into a competitive market.

BUILDING AN INTERESTING BRAND: A popular strategy for entering a saturated and/or competitive market, as the 'new kid on the block' you have less money, less influence, and less experience than the older boys. Trying to keep up with them is an almost futile act. You need something unique. Something that only you have that makes others pay attention to you even if you are a rookie in a room full of champions and veterans. This is your brand.

I could list some specific examples but there are just so many! I suppose one of the most well-known is Apple's more stylish branding being used to separate their products from Microsoft's dull ones. Even a Goliath like Microsoft is not safe from an opponent who knows how to stand out from the rest.

You can take the same route as Apple and distinguish your brand visually. You could also just tell your own story. Few consumers think about the people behind brands like Wal-Mart or McDonald's. Instead, they think of how huge those businesses are and how rich the owners and executives must be. Highlighting your status as a small business without a lot of capital can make you far more relatable to the average shopper.

IDENTIFY AND SOLVE A PAIN POINT: There has never been a better time to be alive in history. The best and brightest of us have worked diligently to make every one of us live comfortably. Once deadly diseases are now treatable if not curable. Modern vehicles make travel so easy that plans are being made to explore the solar system. Advancing technology continues to make performing tasks so easy that people are afraid of not having jobs in the near future.

All of the things that cause discomfort are pain points. I mentioned some big ones but there are small ones, too. I can type out this book on a computer because dipping pens in ink that smudged all over the paper was a pain point for writers. The printing press and typewriters were revolutionary even though they were not cures for cancer. Try isolating some minor frustrations and then think of products that can remove them.

Note that when I brought up advancing technology I also included a fear that people have. The solution to what was once a problem can create a new problem. Be on the lookout for innovations that change the way a lot of us live. Those changes can create an environment for a new pain point to develop.

IDENTIFY AND CATER TO PASSIONS: I think this type of opportunity is the easiest to understand. You identify something that a lot of people are interested and provide an additional something that appeals to those people. This is what many people do with blogs and vlogs to start building a following. Someone who wants to travel but is unable to will settle for a virtual escape in the meantime.

Fan merchandise falls under this category, too. You should get permission before reproducing symbols and logos that belong to someone else, but fan art can be sold legally as of the time that I am writing this. If you are an artist, slap that art onto clothes, mugs, and bags if you think the fanatics will buy them.

Not an artist? Well somebody has to supply all the clothes, mugs, and bags to be printed over. Creative types are all about that passion and you can take advantage of that. It is also possible that one person can do all of the above. If you share the same passion as your clients then a lot of this work could feel more like an addictive hobby. Cater responsibly.

LOOK FOR AN OPPORTUNITY GAP: As smartphones became ubiquitous in the early 2000s, the people ran into a problem. They wanted to take photos of themselves using their phones. However, it was near impossible to get the right angle and lighting while holding the device only an arm's length away. Friendly bystanders were a godsend but could not be relied upon at all times. The people cried out for a solution and the market answered their cries with the Selfie Stick.

That is how you take advantage of an opportunity gap. Human beings always want 'more' regardless of how much they already have. People in houses want bigger houses. People who own a car want another car. People who get food delivered to their homes want faster delivery. There will always be a demand for something new to make living just a little bit easier. Provide something to achieve that goal and you will have plenty of business.

Opportunity gaps are like minor pain points; nobody complains because they are more of an inconvenience than a cause of stress. Discovering one will take research and awareness. You can ask the people around you about the products they use and if they feel like something is missing when they use them.

UTILIZE YOUR OWN EXPERIENCE: Young entrepreneurs are still young people. They are optimistic and ambitious with little to lose and so much to gain. Older people tend to move with caution and lower expectations. One of your biggest assets, as you age, is your experience. Wisdom cannot be bought or stolen and its value is priceless.

The more work experience and expertise you have in a field, the more of an advantage you have others who are entering it. Writing and publishing your own book should not only generate some income but also show others in the field that you know what you are talking about. As a consequence of that, any products you sell in the future will stand out because of your reputation.

Your choice of media does not have to be in writing. You can make videos or host seminars. The objective is just to make it known that you are an authority in your field. Not feeling confident? Do it regardless! If even one of your industry insights is unique it might be enough to establish a following.

CAPITALIZE ON TRENDS: This one is tricky. The idea is similar to that of finding opportunities in keywords. A trend has to be identified early and capitalized on immediately for the best results. Being the second person to catch on might not be good enough depending on consumer demand and how long the trend lasts.

Let us pretend that I have identified what I believe to be a trend. How do I confirm this? The most straightforward way is to buy a small amount of whatever I think I need to sell and put it up for sale.

If sales are anything less than stellar then either I am too late or I have not identified a trend at all. If it really is trendy I should see a significant amount of that product sold in a couple of days. The next step is to buy a lot more of that trendy product and make sure consumers know what I have done so.

TIP: I would like you to take a moment and reflect on your mindset. It is the one thing that will keep you going. Set it right, and no obstacle will deter you from that handsome Amazon deposit in your bank account.

Thanks to this online business, I was able to quit my day job and work for myself. Eventually, I reached a net profit level in the six-figure range and I stabilized there. I can give you all the details of my success in *"Amazon FBA Mastery Coaching: The Definitive Guide to Learn the Secret Way to Sell Fulfillment By Amazon"* which is available at Amazon.com.

CHAPTER 14
DROPSHIPPING

When it comes to earning money, people look at various business models. If you want to do something but still keep your regular job, you have a few options. Dropshipping is a process that is recommended by several websites. The problem with drop shipping is the number of responsibilities that it involves. Unlike affiliate marketing where you promote a product for a business and hold no responsibility whatsoever for the quality of the product delivered, drop shipping holds you responsible for a faulty or bad quality product. You always need to be available to customers and provide them with support and assistance. Also, you need to go back and forth with the merchant and your buyer, which takes a lot of time. In its true sense, affiliate marketing is passive income, because once you create your blog page and promote it on your end, all you need to do is sit back and relax while customers continue shopping through your affiliate network.

It may take you a while to establish a strong blog and generate traffic to it but once this is done, you will automatically have people coming to your website or blog and going through your network to buy products.

CHAPTER 15
YOUTUBE VIDEOS

In addition to Facebook and Instagram, YouTube marketing has also gained a lot of popularity. There are various businesses that prefer to share videos in order to enhance marketing efforts, and the best way to share these videos is by sharing them on YouTube. The reason YouTube marketing is more effective when it comes to videos is that you can rest assured someone has watched your video when it's placed at the start as opposed to when the ad is placed in between a video that they are watching. YouTube is responsible for creating a lot of awareness for various businesses, and it also is effective when you are a startup. If you have little or no credibility, and you want to create mass awareness in a short time span, YouTube is probably your best bet.

As all of us know, YouTube belongs to Google – a company that has taken up most of the market today. With over a billion registered subscribers, people spend hours on YouTube each day watching videos across various genres. No matter what kind of videos you are looking for, you are sure to find them on YouTube. This gives you the leverage to add your advertisement to videos that are related to your business in some way or the other. When it comes to behavioral targeting, it is very effective to do it when you are doing it through YouTube. This is because you will find videos of all genres here and you will be able to relate your business to one of these genres.

YOUTUBE MARKETING STRATEGIES

Promoting your business on YouTube is great, but like all social media platforms, you need to begin with a strategy in mind. Without a strong strategy, your efforts on YouTube will go down the drain. There are various goals people have when they advertise on YouTube, and it depends on the nature of your business. If you are a personality or a public figure, the only reason you'll advertise on YouTube is to get more visibility, if you are a business and you want people to come to visit your website, then that needs to be your goal. There are also e-Commerce websites that would like to sell products, and these videos could simply include a 'buy now' link that directs a potential customer straight to their sales page to help increase sales. Your strategy needs to be based on your end goal and why you are advertising on YouTube in the first place.

CHAPTER 16
SOCIAL MEDIA INFLUENCER

The first question that you really need to ask yourself when you're laying down the foundation for your personal brand is whether you're capable of becoming an influencer in your own niche or not. For one to be able to influence people from a specific industry or niche, the influencer needs to have a tremendous amount of knowledge and information about the product or industry in general. Followers and fans should be so impressed by the profound knowledge of the influencer that they can directly have an impact on them and influence their thought processes. A person who is capable of being an influencer in their own niche is sort of like the expert of the industry. They should be able to provide proper guidance to his followers and fans. As an industry expert, they will share their experiences on all possible platforms, including articles, videos, social media, books, conferences, personal interactions, pamphlets, interviews, and so on.

DO YOU HAVE THE CAPABILITIES TO PROMOTE YOUR OWN PRODUCTS?

Not every manufacturer goes out on the market to promote his or her own products. There are some individuals who have the potential and power to market and promote their own products, while there are others who don't. You need to find out for yourself whether you have the right tools to influence people to invest in the products that you have to offer. Try to promote your products yourself a few times, and if you see a rise in sales and general inquiries for the product, you might just be the influencer that your company needs. If you see no increase in sales or maybe even a drop-in sale, maybe you should leave the promotion and branding to the professionals.

CHAPTER 17
EMAIL MARKETING
A POWERFUL LEAD GENERATION TOOL!

Another strategy that I see that not all bloggers are exploring is email marketing. For this to work to its fullest, it is essential that you have a list of correctly obtained emails, which is to let your own readers subscribe to your blogs or websites.

Many may think that Email Marketing does not have the same conversion strength as blog banners, but what I can say over the course of time exploring this type of advertising is that it converts more than the banners people insert in their blogs. Of course, for the success of these campaigns, it is necessary to respect the ethical limits of sending emails, not making our readers end up unsubscribing from your mailing list.

INCENTIVES AND SOCIAL NETWORKS

This is another subject that I think is very little explored by bloggers and webmasters. Social networks are places that move almost all people who access the internet, making the possibilities of generating leads very large if well explored. Also, the people who will see your campaigns on social networks are your friends or acquaintances, who know your reputation and what makes your reporting power great. Of course, to get feedback from this type of disclosure, you need to have a well-connected and influential profile on social networks.

UNDERSTAND THE MOST PROFITABLE REGIONS OF YOUR BLOG OR WEBSITE

Following the concept of working lead generation campaigns with recommendations within articles, there are also the articles that people publish that are specific about a particular product or service. This has a high conversion power, but one cannot abuse this and make their blogs strictly "commercial." In this case, it is important to understand the most viewed sites in our blogs.

I would suggest dividing your articles into 3 blogs, where the first block consists of the first paragraphs with an introduction about what will be treated, the second is composed by the middle of the article and the third by the final part of the article. With this, you can clearly say that the links that have the highest chance of conversion are those that are in the FINAL of the first block.

CHAPTER 18
COUPON WEBSITE

One of the easiest ways to increase your income today is through discount websites. These discount websites offer coupons that can be turned into income by anyone who knows how to use them. Since making money online is becoming harder nowadays due to the huge competition in all niche markets, knowing how to make money from discount coupons is a great opportunity.

Today, coupons have proven to be one of the easiest ways to make money online, and especially nowadays, that niche is still low in competitiveness. You can quickly create a discount coupon site even if you do not know about programming or design.

Discount coupon sites allow your users to receive discount coupons for multiple online stores. Users can use these discount codes to redeem unique and specific prices for that online store. So there are many online search prospects for "Discount Coupon." If you provide discount coupons to visitors to your online space, they will always receive the discounts available. People use these coupons to get a specific discount at that online store for wanted products, which always takes them back to their space. Once they complete your purchase online on your site, you will receive credit for this sale, and this store will send you your commission on your payment schedule.

Whenever you use a coupon or offer a link, the coupon sites earn a percentage on the purchase. This amount is paid by affiliate networks such as Lomadee, Zanox and Afilio. To register on these platforms is free, just have a website or blog to enable registration. The platforms have direct partnerships with the major retail networks and share the earnings of the sales indication with the affiliates who generated the nomination. Coupon sites use the links provided by these affiliate networks that have code that identifies the site.

These commissions vary according to the type of business. Example, in airfare usually is 1 to 2% in electronics on average 4% and so on. Each product type has a different margin. The harder the generation of business, the higher the commission.

If you are ready to start your own website and earn money with a discount coupon, you need the following items ready before you start increasing your income:

1. Register your domain name and host

2. Register name from the domain to your virtual space is the first step to start working to make money with coupons.

3. Apply as an affiliate

4. Install your coupon and theme plugin

Now your discount website is ready to be marketed. You will need to bring visitors to it, and there are innumerable ways to do it.

Write high-quality articles on "How to get a discount for a specific online store" and post those articles in some article directory with a link back to your discount coupon site. Join online forums where your audience is present. Help them get discounts on their desired online store with the forum posts. Create small but appealing videos on topics like "How to get discounts on wallmart.com?" And upload your video on YouTube by inserting your site link at the top of your video description.

With the above tips, making money from discount coupon websites has never been so easy, making you get the best for your income at the end of the month!

SECTION

TWO

LEARNING PROPERTY BASED METHODS TO EARN PASSIVE INCOME

CHAPTER 19
REAL ESTATE INVESTOR

This is one of the ancient and most well-known ways to generate passive income. The question remains on similar lines here too - How to make money in the real estate market?

As all of us know, there are two ways to make money from real estate:

1. Buy a property as an investment medium and then sell it, pocketing profits.

2. Owning and thus being able to secure a rent income.

Both alternatives look good, do not they? But what if you had a third option? One that would possibly make you profit much more than the previous ones, through expressive returns. Many people do not know what it really takes to make good gains. With the lack of good recommendations of truth, they end up being limited to the common - to buy or rent.

This alternative to buying or renting is precisely having a portfolio of Real Estate Funds. The mechanism is quite simple. You "buy" a part of a property and receive a rent corresponding to that part. For the sake of discussion in this and the following paragraphs, Countries are experiencing a downturn in the real estate market. And, buying low can mean big fortunes in the future. We are at the height of the rebates in a market that had long since stagnated. The timing is ideal and can boost various ways of investing. It's okay for you to be adept at buying or renting a classic. But in exact moments like this, you need to know the different possibilities to become a better investor of your money. And most importantly: invest safely.

Such guides and research videos and content can be found on almost every market, which again emphasizes the point that you may not have prior knowledge of this sector, but you can surely earn great returns if you invest wisely and safely.

As previously said, I started my entrepreneurial career online with a business called Amazon FBA and my life has completely changed in just twelve short months.

Thanks to this online business, I was able to quit my day job and work for myself.

But while I was more than pleased with my success, I realized that I needed to differentiate my business in order to continue to grow my financial security the way I wanted to. This is a fundamental requirement for continued growth and development. I needed another source of passive income because economic stability depends on having multiple sources of income.

After researching several opportunities, I knew that real estate investing would give me the perfect opportunity to continue to grow my wealth. I soon learned that even though I already have a six-figure income, it would not be needed for me to invest in real estate. I found so many ways to begin my career with little or no money down.

You will find many options available in the real estate market—opportunities that will give you a regular source of income for years to come. With the proper tools and techniques, which I intend to give you, you will be able to enjoy the exact same kind of success that I am currently enjoying in my life. With this knowledge, the only other thing you will need is to have a positive mindset and be prepared to succeed. This book is about the correct way to buy and maintain rental real estate properties. There is the right way and the wrong way to do it, just like any other field. I want to show you the right way to make money in this field. You can't just find a listing and assume it will be perfect. But there are ways to find good listings and this book will show you how to do it. This book will show you what a good rental property is, how to find it, and how to get it. And yes, there are ways to acquire property even if you don't have down payment money available or if you already have multiple mortgages on the books. Anything is possible. I will show you through my experiences how to be successful in the rental real estate market.

Successful real estate investing will give you everything you need to achieve present and future financial security. You will learn the basic of the business and what you need to know to grow your own empire and enjoy the same success that I am currently enjoying. You will learn how to overcome challenges and be able to anticipate issues that you can easily avoid on your path to success.

There are many reasons someone might choose this field as one in which they can make money—now and in the future. One of the most important reasons, at least in the beginning, is that you can start with one rental property while you continue to work at your regular job. Because let's be honest; most people can't just quit their day job the moment they buy their first rental property. Getting into the market this way will mean that you will need to work nights and weekends on the rental property but if it is a necessary way to get started, then that is what you will do. Once you have several properties and you are enjoying regular cash flow then you might be able to drop down to part-time or to quit altogether. Be patient; it will happen.

The real estate market is relatively easy to learn and that includes rental property investing. There are many available resources, both in the library and online, that will give you the answer to any question you might have. There are many people who are more than willing to share the things they have learned with those who are just starting out.

Buying rental property allows you to manage your monetary investment directly if you chose to. Some people will hire a property manager but if this is your full-time job and you want to be a hands-on kind of landlord, this is the business to do it in. And if you enjoy being in charge and controlling events, then rental property is the market for you because you are responsible directly for what happens to your investment. It is your responsibility to check out the property before you buy it to make sure it is a good investment. It is your job to make certain the property is suitable for and attractive to potential renters. The preferred way for many people to do this is to manage the business themselves.

Of all the things that people can give up in life, people will always need somewhere to live. Not everyone can afford to become a homeowner because even if they have the down payment they may not have the income to be able to afford the regular upkeep of a house. Not everyone wants to be a homeowner. For whatever reason you can think of, there will always be people who need to rent somewhere to live. And you can provide this place.

Rental property is real; it is a tangible investment. You can see it right in front of you. If you make an improvement on the property, then you can see how much better it looks afterward. Rental property may occasionally drop in value but it will always come back up and while it is rented to someone you will continue to make money. And you can use other people's money to grow your investments. Other people will help with down payments. Other people will pay you rent money to live in your house.

And along with the nearly constant cash flow, you will also enjoy tax breaks as the owner of rental property. There are many tax laws that make a favorable environment for property owners. For instance, the interest expense that you pay along with your monthly mortgage payment is tax deductible. Your operating expenses are also deductible. This means that your depreciation, insurance, property taxes, and operating expenses are all deductible. This is an extra layer of savings that will be much enjoyed at tax time.

Buying real estate to use as rental property is a fantastic investment if you are willing to do what you need to do to be successful. You will get amazing returns if you just learn the processes. The best thing about rental property is that they become better investments the longer that you own them. You make cash flow from rental properties every month, money that comes to you on a regular basis. Your cash flow will naturally increase over time because the rate of rental payments will increase but your mortgage payment will remain steady, thus making your cash flow increase on a regular basis. When the mortgage is paid off the cash flow will significantly increase.

And by purchasing rental property you are building equity for your future, including money for your retirement. The monetary difference between what you owe and what the house is worth is the equity. Since the value of the property will increase over time as the amount that you owe becomes less, your equity is always increasing. And once the properties are paid off, the rental income will provide a nice regular source of income for your later years.

Investing in rental property has many overall benefits and will prove to be a great source for passive income. Your potential for profit will increase because the value of rental property increases with the increasing demand for property. There are several important advantages to investing in real estate for rental property. As long as you go into this with your eyes wide open and a ready mindset, you will be successful.

Investors are able to find rental properties that are available for sale by using many different techniques. If you rely on a wide variety of resources to help you find properties, then you will be giving yourself the best overall possible chance to find the investment property that is perfect for you.

Networking is one way that many people use to find rental properties. This method will give you access to properties that the general public may not know about yet. People are often hearing about their friends and neighbors who are thinking about selling their homes. This could give you the inside track on a new property to purchase. Professional contacts such as attorneys or contractors might also have information regarding other properties for sale.

Some people prefer to join investment clubs that are groups of people who spend their time looking for and talking about real estate. These clubs may have a small annual membership fee of a few hundred dollars but that can be well worth it for the chance to find new properties to buy. And the membership fee is most likely tax deductible as a business expense. You might also belong to a group of other property investors or landlords who will hear about available properties that they themselves might not be interested in.

Realtors are a great source of information regarding properties to buy for rental properties. After all, the realtor's job is to locate properties for sale for people who want to buy them and to locate people to buy the properties their clients want to sell. You can easily make an appointment with a realtor to look at individual listings. Or you can drive through a particular area that you might want to own property in to see if any properties are for sale. If you find any, you can call the realtor listed on the sign and make an appointment to see the house. You can also check out open houses where you can actually go through the house and look at it with less intimate contact with the realtor since hopefully many people will be viewing the house at the same time you are.

Banks often have a backlog of properties available that are for sale because they have been foreclosed on. Banks like to sell these properties because they do not bring in any income for the bank sitting empty and unused. These properties are generally listed with a realtor eventually but if you can catch a listing before it goes to the realtor then you can avoid paying the realtor's fees and this will save you money.

Do not overlook the newspaper as a valuable source of information. Many people get their news online these days but there are certain things that will still be found in the newspaper in black and white print. In the classified section you will find notices of foreclosures or sheriff's sales. A foreclosure sale is held when a lending institution has reacquired a property from an owner who could not or did not make their monthly mortgage payment. The lender will take allow all interested people to tour the property and then they will take bids for buying the property, either during a live auction or by sealed bid. The bidder with the best bid wins. These properties are generally sold for the value of the note owing on the house so it is possible to pick up a good property for less money. These are sometimes referred to as sheriff's sales. These will be listed in the newspaper because they must be publicly announced.

Buying property at a foreclosure sale or a sheriff's sale is a great way to find a good deal on a property for investment purposes. These are local sales held by the county government. These sales are open to the public. Anyone who wants to bid on a property must have the funds in place prior to the sale and you must have proof that the funds are available. Property listings, either online or in the newspaper, will include the address and description of the property and the listing will also include the upset price. This is the minimum amount that the plaintiff (the one who is selling the property) will take as a bid for the property. It is a good idea to do a complete coverage title search on any property you might want to buy. Searching the title for discrepancies will tell you if there are any liens against the house, such as contractor liens, utility company liens, or even liens from any source that collects tax money. Liens are lawsuits placed on a property when that particular bill has not been paid by the homeowner. So if you hire someone to put new gutters on your house and you never pay him, he can file a lien against your property. These liens may or may not be satisfied (paid off) by the proceeds from the sale. If they are not, then the new owner is responsible for paying them.

The amount of money that you bid on a property depends on two things: how much is the minimum required bid and how much are you willing to spend. You must bring a certified check, also known as a cashier's check or an official check, for the down payment. You will need to know what percentage of the purchase price the down payment must be. It might be ten percent, fifteen percent, or twenty percent. So if you are willing to pay at the most $200,000 for the property then you must bring a check for twenty thousand dollars on a ten percent down, thirty thousand dollars on a fifteen percent down, and forty thousand dollars on a twenty percent down. Closing depends on the term of the local county sheriff's office but it is usually within thirty days. That means in thirty days from the auction you must have your financing arranged and have taken possession of the house.

When you are ready to buy your first property you need to decide what your personal criteria will be for the property. Making this list is like making a shopping list for the grocery store. Deciding before your search exactly what you are looking for will help keep you focused on the search so that you will be able to find the kind of properties that you are looking for. When you are making your list be sure to think about all of the attributes you would like a house to have. If you are in a large city and looking in the suburbs, which city would you prefer? Which neighborhood would you like to buy into? How big will the lot be and how many square feet will be in the house. Do you want to buy move-in ready or a fixer-upper? What is the CAP rate? How much cash flow can you expect to receive? What is the potential for appreciation?

CAP rate refers to the term capitalization rate, which is the amount of money you would expect to receive from a property over the period of one year. It will help you to determine whether or not a particular property is a good investment. The CAP rate is the ratio of property asset value to net operating income. So let's say you are looking at two different properties that are already set up as rental units. Both properties are rented for ninety-five percent of the year.

Property A	Property B
Value $500,000	Value $600,000
Occupancy rate 95%	Occupancy rate 95%
Gross rental income $60,000	Gross rental income $72,000
Operating expenses $25,000	Operating expenses $32,000

The first step in the equation is to multiply the gross rental income by the occupancy rate:

Property A: 95% x $60,000 = $57,000

Property B: 95% x $72,000 = $68,400

The next step is to subtract the operating expenses:

Property A: $57,000 - $25,000 = $32,000

Property B: $68,400 - $32,000 = $36,400

Now you have the Net Operating Income (NOI). This is the yearly income that is generated by a rental property counting all of the income that is generated from operations and subtracting the expenses that come from operating the property. Divide the NOI number by the current value of the property to get the CAP rate:

Property A: $32,000/$500,000 = 0.064

Property B: $36,400/$600,000 = 0.060

Since the CAP rate is always expressed as a percentage, now multiply each number by one hundred:

Property A: 0.064 x 100 = 6.4% CAP rate

Property B: 0.060 x 100 = 6% CAP rate

These two properties have a similar CAP rate. The determining factor in this example would be some other consideration, such as sales price or location. The figures for the operating expenses, rental income, and occupancy rate can be obtained from the realtor.

An acceptable CAP rate falls somewhere between four percent and ten percent. The CAP rate should just be used as an indicator of profitability while considering other factors. Obviously if the CAP rate falls out of these percentages then the property might not make you the money you desire. You also need to consider local demand, inventory that is available in the area, and the type of property this one is specifically. As an example, a CAP rate of four percent might be quite normal in areas of high demand such as New York City and California. But in an area where the demand is lower, such as an area that is going through regeneration or in a rural area, the normal CAP rate might be ten percent or even higher.

Most buyers look for a higher CAP rate, which means the price to purchase the property is rather low when compared to the net operating income. Unfortunately, a lower CAP rate usually represents a lower risk property where a higher CAP rate usually means a property with a higher risk. A property that has a higher CAP rate might be located in an area that doesn't have much opportunity for regular rental increases or where property does not appreciate as well as it does in other areas. As an investor you will need to weigh all of these factors when deciding on a property to purchase.

One thing to remember when comparing CAP rates is to compare rates on similar properties. This just means to compare properties that are similar to each other and are in similar areas. An investment property that is a multifamily rental unit will probably have a CAP rate that is much lower than a commercial building that is full of retail tenants. This means that the multifamily unit will probably be an investment of lower reward than the commercial building but it will also probably be a lower risk. This is because in times of economic downturn people still need to live somewhere, where retail customers might close up and move away.

CAP rates are affected by four factors:

2.1 INTEREST RATES: Property values typically fall when interest rates rise. When the rates rise, the debt ratio usually rises which will mean a decrease in net cash flow so lower CAP rates come from rising interest rates. The rent will remain the same but if the interest rate is higher then you will not make as large of a profit.

2.2 AVAILABLE INVENTORY: This term refers to the number of properties that are available in one particular area. If the inventory is lower the demand for property will be higher, this will lead to properties with a lower CAP rate.

2.3 ASSET CLASS: This is the factor that tells what type of property it is, like a commercial property, a single-family dwelling, an apartment building, etc. Residential properties usually have lower CAP rates than commercial properties because you can charge a higher rent to a commercial tenant.

2.4 LOCATION: The local economy and property demand is driven by the location of the property. A property in a more desirable location will have a higher value and higher rents, which will affect the overall CAP rate.

CAP rate is only one way to evaluate properties when deciding which property is the better investment. You should really be prepared to consider several factors when deciding which property will be the best investment property for you to buy. Doing this will give you a better, more well-rounded picture of the property and whether it has a reasonable potential to be a good investment for you. Particularly if the property needs to be remodeled or is vacant you will probably want to use extra tools in order to evaluate it. Here are several ways to make an evaluation of a potential investment property:

2.4.1 RETURN ON INVESTMENT (ROI): Usually ten percent or more is considered to be a good ROI for any real estate investment property. ROI is determined by dividing your total investment into your annual return. Annual return is determined by subtracting the amount of expenses from the total rental income.

2.4.2 THE PERCENTAGE RULE: This is the one percent rule or the two percent rule, both are used equally. This guide says that the monthly gross income should be at least one percent, or two percent, of the price of the purchase. If the monthly gross income is more than one percent of the price of the purchase, then the property usually will have a positive flow of cash.

2.4.3 GROSS RENTAL YIELD: Take the collected annual rent by the total cost of the property and then multiply by one hundred; the higher the number the better the yield. The total cost of the property will include any renovation costs, closing costs, and the purchase price.

2.4.4 CASH FLOW: See if the expected monthly rental income covers the monthly costs that will include the homeowner's association fees, utilities, taxes, insurance, and mortgage payment. If the rental amount collected exceeds the amount of expenses, then the cash flow is positive.

2.4.5 PER-UNIT PRICE: In a multifamily unit or a commercial building take the purchase price and divide it by the number of units in the building. This will give you a price per unit so that you can determine if the unit is worth that price based on its cosmetic appearance and overall usefulness.

2.4.6 COMPARABLE PROPERTIES: Get the figures from the last three to six months of the sale price, rental rates, and occupancy rates for buildings that are similar to the building you are considering purchasing. When comparing properties, they need to be similar in size, have amenities that are similar, and be the same types of properties.

When considering the other factors that are listed on your particular list of criteria, remember that you have the right to be as demanding as you want to be. No one can tell you what your particular investment should look like. Just remember that if you are too narrow in your consideration, you might not have very much inventory to choose from. But when you are able to specify the particular criteria of the rental property, you want to own it will be easy for you to search for a property to buy. And in knowing what you want to buy you will be better able to tell other people what you are looking for. Just telling people "Hey, I'm looking for rental properties to buy" will probably get you a nice smile. But telling people "Hey, I'm looking for a three-bedroom, two bath, single family home on a one-acre lot in the Millwood are of town" will probably get you some action on your request.

The most important part of the package of criteria that you will assemble is the financial part of your package. If the financial component of the deal does not add up to a profit, that property will probably not be a good deal. Usually a real estate listing will not tell you the information that you might find important to know about the financial information of a property. While you might be able to calculate an estimation for the amount of rental income a property might bring in, you will not immediately know how much cash flow the property brings in every month, if the property is overpriced, or exactly how much you should offer on the property. And even though you might love working a spreadsheet, it will not make sense to work one up for each property you are looking at. This is when you learn to use the "rules."

The 'rules' comes from the term "rules of thumb." These rules will give a buyer a rapid way to evaluate the financial health of a property. Using these rules is not exact and should not be the only consideration used to determine the worth of a property. These rules can help you quickly decide if a property may or may not be worth pursuing.

We have already discussed the one percent or two percent, rule. This rule is that whichever percent you use the monthly rental income should be that percentage of the purchase price. So using this rule a house that is priced at $100,000 should bring either $1000 or $2000 in rent each month. This is a very simple way to compare properties but it can let you know whether or not a particular property needs more investigation. Using the rule from the other way works like this: if the monthly rent is $500, you would not pay more than $50,000 for the house at the rate of one percent.

Then there is the fifty percent rule. This rule will help you to somewhat accurately tell how much your monthly expenses will be on the property. This rule is that fifty percent of your monthly income will be used for expenses on the property and this does not include the monthly mortgage payment. Since most real estate listings will tell you how much monthly income comes from the property you can easily get a good estimate of your monthly cash flow. Take the monthly income and divide that number in half. So half will go to expense and the other half needs to be enough to cover the mortgage. Anything left over is cash flow. The fifty percent for expenses will need to cover rehab costs for tenant turnover, management costs, utilities, vacancies, taxes, insurance, repairs, and some savings for the larger cost items like repaving or a new roof.

The last rule that is often used is the seventy percent rule. This rule is used by investors to determine quickly the maximum amount of the purchase price that you should offer. This number is based on the after-repair value (ARV) of the property and is used for those properties that will require a major renovation before they are ready to rent. This rule says you should pay no more than seventy percent of the value of the property after repairs minus the costs of the repairs. Use the following as an example:

This property needs extensive repair before it can be rented. After renovation it should sell for about two hundred thousand dollars. It needs around thirty-five thousand dollars in repair work. So to use the seventy percent rule you would multiply two hundred thousand by seventy percent to get one hundred forty thousand and then subtract the thirty-five thousand for the repair costs. That means the most you should pay for this property would be one hundred five thousand dollars.

Keep in mind that the rules of them are only used to give an efficient and quick way to screen a property. Any property that falls far out of line of one of the rules is probably not worth investing any more time or attention and especially not money.

When you are ready to buy a property, you will certainly not hand over a check and get keys in return. It does not work as quickly as it seems to work on television. There is a set process that is followed every time you purchase a property, no matter what type of property it is.

So let's begin at the point where you have found the property you want and you are ready to buy it. Your very first step is to decide how you are going to finance this purchase. This just means that you already have in mind a definite idea of how you are going to pay for this property. You need to be pre-approved by the lender if you are going to use a loan from any financial institution. If you have the funds and want to do an all cash offer, then those funds need to be liquid and available immediately. Liquid means they are sitting in a bank account or a credit union account and you can walk in the door and get an official check for the amount you need. If you are planning to use the proceeds from the sale of the jewelry Aunt Martha left you in her will, then that jewelry needs to have been already sold and the money put into an account. Money is liquid, property is an asset. Most real estate agents as well as anyone who has been buying real estate for any length of time, will recommend that you have your financing in place first before you ever go looking for property. If you find a great deal the chances are good that someone else found that same great deal, and whoever brings the money to the table first wins. So have your choice of financing ready.

Now you want you make an offer. This offer is made on paper, usually on a pre-printed form that has all of the correct legal terms on it. You will also determine the amount of time the offer will be good for. You and your real estate agent (if you are using one) will simply fill in the blanks and then it will go to the seller or their real estate agent. The seller's real estate agent will take it to their client and together they will discuss the offer and determine if it is acceptable to them. If you are not using an agent, you can find appropriate forms online but have your attorney look over the form before you submit it to make sure there are no errors.

When making an offer you do not need to offer the sale price. Perhaps the property needs renovation and the seventy percent rule calculations you did came up with a purchase price lower than what the seller is asking for. Sometimes sellers will ask for a price higher than what the property is worth to see how much they can get. It is perfectly acceptable to offer less than the sales price. Also in your offer you will put any contingencies that you have. These are stipulations that must occur before you will agree to buy the property. You may require any number of contingencies in the offer:

2.5 HOME INSPECTION: This will allow you to hire a home inspector who is certified by your state to do home inspections. While home inspectors can't possibly see all the problems a property might have, they can certainly see problems that might cause a hefty repair bill like the need for foundation work or a new work.

Be prepared to be excited and energized by what you will see in this book. This book will fill you with knowledge and excitement and everything you need to be successful in the rental property real estate market.

You will quickly learn how much I love the world of rental property real estate. Since I have discovered how easy it is to make money at this and how much fun it actually is I really don't want to stop. I originally got into this business as an addition to my portfolio. I was already enjoying success with my Amazon online business but I knew I needed to diversify if I wanted to keep growing my wealth and my future possibilities. So I chose real estate rental property.

I can give the all the details of my success in *"Rental Property Investing: Secrets of a Real Estate Building Empire"* which is available on Amazon.com.

CHAPTER 20
REAL ESTATE CROWDFUNDED

Buying to lease has seen a resurgence in recent times. For those who have the ability to borrow or already have enough capital, real estate investment for rent seems very attractive, especially when we compare it with greedy savings rates and shareholder market volatility. What also attracts in this investment is the recurrence of the revenues and the passive character, that is, you need to do little to receive your rents after the initial investment.

Here I must stop you once to draw your attention: beware of low-interest rates! They are volatile in nature and you must to do the math to see if you can afford to invest if the rates go up. However, to help you, I have mentioned some essential tips you can keep in mind to invest more successfully in the lease market (includes crowdfunded properties).

1. INVESTIGATE THE MARKET
If you are new to the real estate market, it is important that you become aware of the risks and opportunities. Make sure that buying for lease is the investment you are looking for. Your money may be able to perform better elsewhere. However, buying for lease means that you will have your capital tied up on a property that may lose value.

Investing in real estate involves committing hundreds of thousands of your currency to a property and usually requires a mortgage. When home prices rise, it is possible to make large leveraged gains on your home equity loan, but when your assets fall, they are hit, and the mortgage remains the same.

Investment in real estate has been extremely profitable for many people, both in terms of income and in terms of capital gains, but it is essential that you enter it with your eyes wide open, identifying the potential advantages and disadvantages. If you know someone who invested in leasing, ask him about his experience - the wrinkles he won, the hair he lost, everything ...

The more knowledge you have and the more research you do, the more likely your investment will be worth it.

2. CHOOSE AN ATTRACTIVE AREA

Attractive does not mean cheap or expensive. Attractive means a place where people would like to live, and this may be due to several reasons. What is the neighborhood in your city that has a special appeal? If you live in a suburban area, what are transports like? Where are good schools for young families? Where do the students want to live?

These neighborhoods have more appeal when it comes to guaranteeing income (especially for temporary rent), but if you look for absolute return (valuation of the property plus income), you may be looking for neighborhoods still in revitalization. In the end, you have to look at whether the property you can and want to buy is in a place where people would like to live. These questions may seem too simplistic, but they are probably the most important aspect of an investment for lease.

3. DO THE MATH

Before you go running to the computer to look at specialty sites for a home, sit down with a pen and paper and note the cost of the homes you are looking for and the income you want to get. Better yet, the first question you need to answer is: what is the fair value of a home? One of the most common mistakes for renters is to forget to incorporate expenses when calculating the cap rate or the valuation.

While it is normal to value the price of housing in the long term, experts say that they should invest to generate income, not for capital gains in the short term. In short, to compare the values of different properties, you must use the formula of the cap rate. For example, if a property has operating results of € 10,000 and the property value is € 200,000, then it has a cap rate of 5%.

That is if a house that costs € 300,000 generates a cap rate of 6% (if everything else is constant) it is a better investment to rent than the cheapest house (cap rate = 5%). The absolute value is your limit, but the important thing is to calculate what income you can get from the property versus the house price (relative value).

4. THE IMPORTANCE OF MANAGING EXPENDITURE

In this first part, we explained how to analyze the earning potential of real estate. Now let's talk about how the return potential affects the value of it. Let's talk about a concept which can work wonders for you in this market and in analyzing and calculating what your returns will be.

An important concept which helps a lot while investing and calculating returns in this sector is - multiples.

When a baker wants to trade his bakery, the tricky way to come up with a value would be to hire a specialist to project his cash flows, establish a discount rate that would be appropriate to the risk, and thus get a negotiation. This is not practical, and bakers prefer to take the easy way out. With many years of transactions, he has established a practice of trading bakeries based on multiples of annual sales.

So if you buy bakeries for your annual turnover or maybe, if it's a great quality bakery 1.3 times - and so on. What is important is that every experienced baker knows, more or less, how profitable a bakery is. Then it is implied that the business has the potential to generate a certain profit and therefore, in an indirect way, a projection is being defined cash flow and a discount rate.

Negotiation flows much more easily because billing is verifiable. Just count the money that is in the cash register every day for a month. The comparison is also easier since to know if a bakery is cheap or expensive, just observe the multiple required, starting with the reference at once the billing. In the same way that the baker sells his business based on a billing multiple, shopping center companies negotiate their business on a multiple basis.

In the case in question, the most widely used multiple is the capitalization rate (discussed above).

Cap rate = Operating Result / Property Value

The mergers and acquisitions market is always disclosing recent transactions, and all of them give us a good idea of the current cap rate.

CHAPTER 21
AIRPORT PARKING INVESTOR

HOW TO ASSEMBLE A PARKING LOT AND MAKE MONEY WITH THE GAP To set up a parking lot, business owners should consider the market for the deal. Investing in parking is a tempting business as parking lots keep pace with the growing demand for car space, a business opportunity that comes with increasing numbers of cars and other factors linked to insecurity and a greater number of stolen vehicle incidents. But, beware - Avoid Committing the First Trip Entrepreneurs ERROR!

The need for such types of product in the market is well established with the ever-increasing car space and the steady growth in the buying power and living standards of the people, globally. In addition, you can also see this on a personal front, when you leave your car parked on public roads, you run the risk of burglaries, car predation by passers-by, the car's paint is badly damaged for a long time in the sun, and it is quite uncomfortable to pick up a car on a rainy day. Therefore, parking expenses have become a necessity for those who need to get around with vehicles and keep their car safe.

By all the factors already mentioned above is that this business model has become one of the most profitable and is one of the most sought after. But there are a few things which you still need to keep in mind:

LOCATION TO BUILD A PARKING

It is important that the location of your future parking space is located where there are no vacancies available in the nearby streets, even more so that there are cities where vacancies are offered by the city hall with values well considered. Another tip is to choose a place that is very visible to customers, that everyone has easy access to.

The perfect location of a parking lot that works for workers and not just shoppers is to be close to offices and a lot of shopping outlets. Do a good search in your city and if possible, visit the traffic department to find out the ideal spot. It needs to be visible, have a good possibility of external maneuvering and away from bottled spots of local traffic.

It is important to hire a security company to monitor the vehicles; after all, you will be responsible if something happens. A parking lot may also be located in residential locations serving condominiums, which will be a great business opportunity for entrepreneurs. See also about digital entrepreneurship.

BUSINESS TIPS

To retain customers, parking can be located in condominiums, which may establish a contractual system in which residents can receive rent for, monthly or fortnightly. The business may also work in companies; to carry out the activities in this way, the parking lots must win contracts or bids to render their services in public or private companies. This system also represents a profitable niche market.

Advertising of a parking lot is important, and one of the most effective ways to publicize it is through pamphlets. So we can see that parking can work independently as a company with its own or rented premises, can be located in condominiums of houses and apartments, located in the underground of public or private companies or still operate in shopping centers.

SERVICES OFFERED

In a Non-Location Car Park and hiring system, parking facilities prevail for the quality of services offered. Know that competition is fierce, and only those parking lots that guarantee first-class service and safety will win contracts. One tip to attract customers is to offer car wash and jet labs.

One option for parking services may be those that are exclusive to events. This parking style requires more workforce training that can be hired according to demand, but qualified. These services are usually hired by the event organizer and will require valet service, security and fixed value services for the event.

In addition to the services mentioned above, there are also exclusive services for restaurants or nightclubs, which usually work through contracts between businessmen and nightclubs or restaurants.

STRUCTURE OF A PARKING

The infrastructure of a parking lot should be well-suited so that all your customers feel safe when they leave your car. The tip is to use a complete property or an already empty area in an urban center for purchase or rent. The structure must have an area of at least 1000 m² of covered area and automatic gates. Drop everything and build a good flat area. It will require a medium investment, but it will be a great differential of your enterprise.

In a parking lot they should have signaling devices, valets, demarcation of seats, light poles, guards with guards, ratchets for cards and an office. The floor can be covered with gravel, cement or asphalt, at your discretion. The idea is to have a cover to protect cars and customers from sun and rain. Without a doubt, parking must be automated to provide safety and greater agility in operations. The automation should serve to register customers and thus be able to work through identification cards, barcode readers, ATMs for ticketing and so on.

INVESTMENTS TO BUILD A PARKING

Such parking's require initial investments in facilities, and facility equipment required for production processes such as clock-to-date, lighting, security systems with alarms, electronic gates, furniture and office equipment, telephone and fax. The investments will also be with personnel, automation and computerization, besides the costs and administrative expenses required for the legalization of the company.

With this, the initial investment capital varies according to the size of the enterprise. This amount can be higher or lower, according to the area and value of the property for purchase or rent.

STAFF

The choice of staff to work in the parking lot should consider points such as the ability to serve, driver's license, responsibility and above all, honesty. The work team will be composed of boxes, valets, guards, attendants and administrator who may be the owner / businessman. Depending on the structure of the parking lot, this functional frame may be smaller.

STANDARDS FOR THE PARKING SECTOR

To set up a car park, the entrepreneur must consider that it is necessary to meet certain standards that are part of the legislation that protects the consumer, and also remember that consumers have information about these standards and know their rights.

An important, yet simple thing to remember is the price information that should be clearly visible. Other information that should be visible is the number of spots and whether there are valets.

Important reminder: all parking must have insurance against robbery or theft, according to the legislation of each state or municipality. Otherwise the vehicle would not be totally safe just because it is in the parking lot.

CHAPTER 22
ONLINE MARKET PLACE AIRBNB

WHY IS AIRBNB SO SUCCESSFUL? AND WHAT ARE THE FACTORS YOU NEED TO KEEP IN MIND WHILE TRYING THIS OUT? A lot of people believe that Airbnb started off as a streamlined app with multiple options to reserve hotel rooms, apartments or private rooms that they could rent when they were on vacation. The truth is that the Airbnb founders had their share of struggle, and it started off as something that was listed on Craigslist before they gained popularity. Today, Airbnb listings are no longer allowed on Craigslist, and the business itself has become a $30 billion business with services like no other. The fact that Airbnb manages to cater to the requirements of low budget travelers, as well as those looking for luxury accommodations, makes it accessible to all. The filters available on the platform enable people who love traveling to combine affordability with adventure, thereby making it extremely trendy.

There are a number of people who wonder why Airbnb is such a popular marketplace and what made it grow so tremendously in a short time span. Here we have a look at some of the main reasons why Airbnb is in demand and why it is showing no signs of slowing down any time soon.

IT IS A FREE MARKET!

One of the best things for Airbnb is that it's free to accept for both parties. Unlike most other platforms, users need to register, sign up, and pay a certain fee in order to list their properties on the website. Airbnb allows you to use its platform without charging you any money. If you are a skeptical host and you don't want to invest any money in your business plan, then advertising is one of the last things that should be on your mind.

IT IS AN OPEN PLATFORM

Airbnb has a streamlined platform which is efficient, and you can choose the kind of property that you want to rent out. Whether you have a single bedroom in your house, an entire apartment or you are a hotel owner who's looking to rent out your hotel room; you can still list your property on Airbnb. If you have free space and you are looking for the best way to utilize the space and begin earning money out of it, then you need Airbnb. The hosts on Airbnb have an easy and convenient way to monetize their space that was otherwise just an empty space.

AFFORDABLE

Airbnb gives travelers the option of choosing between really reasonable and affordable properties and luxurious multi-storied apartments that come with a Jacuzzi. This means people can now rent out their properties irrespective of what kind of property they want to list. If you had a financial crisis recently and you are looking for some way to earn money, you don't have to invest in a new property. All you need to do is clear up your spare bedroom, and you can make it Airbnb ready. This is a zero-investment business that you can start, and it can help you get on your feet. There are several families who register on Airbnb when they have financial problems. In fact, that is how the business idea was conceived. Airbnb listings can help people to cope with their financial problems effectively.

SOCIALIZING

One of the reasons people hate staying at a hotel is because it is not warm and welcoming, and you do not feel at home. When you have an Airbnb listing, you can provide people with that warm and homely feeling that they usually crave when they are away from home. The reason why Airbnb works so well is that you interact with the guests as much as they want to, and it helps them feel welcome in a new country, state, or city. Helping them feel welcome not only lowers anxiety levels, but it also gives them the confidence to explore the place a little more. Language isn't something that stops you from communicating with someone because there are amazing translators that are available on your smartphone that can help to communicate with people.

LOCATION

One of the best things about Airbnb is it allows people to search for location-specific apartments or places to rent out. This means that when someone looks for a place in your specific location, your listing will be one of the first listings that will show up. The fact that a person can narrow down their selection to every little detail, including the location and the amenities that are provided, makes it a lot easier for travelers to reserve an Airbnb room rather than look for a cheap hotel or motel. When it comes to choosing a place to rent out on a holiday, flexibility is something that people pay a lot of attention to and Airbnb hosts can be more flexible and understanding than most hotels. This makes it a preferred choice for travellers. It's also more comforting on various levels and this is why people seek that warmth and comfort in the homes they rent out. It is a simple model that works well for both parties.

CHAPTER 23
SHORT TERM LET

As an Airbnb host (or a short term let host. I will be using these terms interchangeably here), you are somebody who is not only earning a passive income, but you are also a business person. The minute you look at your hosting services as a business, that's when you will realize the importance of the quality of services that you provide. As an Airbnb host, you are also required to provide the right management solutions to the business plan that you have come up with. If you have experience in running a business you don't need to stress too much because with a little effort and the right decision, not only will you be able to run your Airbnb apartment like no other, but you will also make sure that you keep the guests as happy as possible. Here is a look at some interesting techniques for business management that comes in handy for an Airbnb host.

USE PROFESSIONAL CLEANING SERVICES

Airbnb hosts tend to try and save money by hiring people that are cheap labor to get the cleaning procedures done in the apartment on a regular basis. This is something you should not compromise on because it is vital that you keep your house sparkling clean throughout the year if you want your guests to stay happy. Spending a little extra money on professional cleaning services makes a lot of sense after every guest checks out in case you don't have a professional cleaner who works for you. Keep in mind that every little nook and corner of the house should be cleaned perfectly, and there should be nothing that is overlooked.

As we have discussed before, there should always be two sets of cleaning that you choose - one which is basic cleaning and the other which is advanced cleaning that needs to take place as soon as the guests leave the space. You should have a dedicated cleaning team working for you because in case one of the training people is sick, you always have a backup. As an Airbnb host, you always look to grow, and the best way to do this is to keep getting positive reviews from people in terms of the cleanliness and hygiene of your space.

OUTSOURCE AS MUCH AS POSSIBLE

Even if you have one house that you have rented out on Airbnb, it could get difficult for you to constantly look after the guests when you have a 9 to 5 job that you need to live up to. In this case, the best thing to do is to outsource most of the jobs to other people. When it comes to cleaning you should always have a dedicated team who will clean your apartment from time to time, who handles the supplies for the apartment on a regular basis, and you should always have someone who looks after the laundry. You will also need a caretaker; however, this is something you can consider later on when you have multiple locations to handle or when your bookings are constantly flowing in.

USE AN ACCOUNTING SOFTWARE

It is very easy for an Airbnb host to believe that they will manage to handle the accounts of the apartment without having to depend on any software to do the calculations for them. However, minor expenses can lead to something major, and you'll end up with no profit in hand unless you have a good accounting system in place. If you don't have one, you can always purchase one at a minimal fee so that you know what the rate you charged for the apartment is, including the taxes and there is a certain profit left even after all the other expenses have been considered. You need to make sure that you list every little detail in this account and it accounts for even a single egg that has been purchased.

SET ASIDE A BUDGET BEFORE YOU START

An Airbnb listing may be free, and you don't have to spend money in order to become an Airbnb host, however there are a number of expenses that come up when you decide to rent your property, and this may be very unexpected, so you need to have a certain amount of money that is set aside. Imagine the first time you rent out your property and the person destroys a few valuables. You could end up in a loss just like that in the business. If you want the show to go on, you must be able to deal with the shortcomings and overcome them as soon as possible.

Before you decide to sign up as an Airbnb host, make sure that you set aside some money that you label as emergency expenses. While this money may not be needed, it's always good to have it handy and it's better to stay prepared in advance. Even with every profit that comes in, you should take out a certain amount of money from it and keep it aside for emergency funds. Later, the same money should be used for additional expenses like renovation or minor repair work that is needed around the house. When you do this, you don't eat into your profit each time you do up the place.

CHAPTER 24
STORAGE PLACE RENTAL

Make money by renting the space left over in your home! The concept of collaborative economy is growing every day and who wins is us, ordinary citizens. Sharing private transportation, office space, renting houses and apartments by season, free time exchange and other options are showing that the future is increasingly collective and less individual. But, have you heard the rental of space at home? That's it. The Wistor is a platform recently launched promoting the encounter between people who have space left at home. They are people who need this space to store their belongings, personal belongings, goods, among others.

HOW DOES HOME SPACE RENT WORK?

Those interested in advertising can make empty rooms available; attics, garages and other diverse spaces that are not being occupied but which can be used to store objects. The interested party sees the ad, and the two are put in touch to combine the details. This is an innovative platform that competes directly with services self-storage. That is, those companies that rent sheds for diverse storage. Generally, renting one of these sheds is expensive and is unobjectionable for those who only need a compact space, are moving and cannot shell out large sums.

In addition, the Wistor also lends a helping hand to anyone who has unproductive space at home, apartment, ranch or other places, giving the opportunity to earn extra income without much effort. Small entrepreneurs, shopkeepers and merchants can also benefit from this collaborative system, not having to rent another property for storage. Another great advantage is that the platform allows the spaces available for rent to be found in the vicinity of those who are looking for it.

LESS PAPERWORK AND BUREAUCRACY

Wistor promises a simple and uncomplicated rent, not requiring paperwork or bureaucracies to make room for rent at home. The settlement is done among the stakeholders in the business.

In an interview with Exame magazine, the co-founder of the Franz Bories platform explains that the site receives 15% commission on the rents on a monthly basis. This fee includes legal support if there are problems such as disagreements and disagreements between who offers the space and who rents, in addition to insurance in the amount of up to $ 1,000.00 in case of damage to the stored objects. According to him, Wistor still does not offer insurance against theft and other contingencies, but this is an idea that is being developed and probably should be put into practice in the future through a partnership with an insurance company.

HOW TO ADVERTISE AN AVAILABLE SPACE AND EARN EXTRA INCOME (EXAMPLE: WISTOR)?

1. Enter the platform wistor.com and enter the region where your space is.

2. Specify the period when your space will be available (days, months, etc.) and also the time the renter will have access to it;

3. Set a value per square meter. Make sure the price is on the average of the other ads;

4. Use photos! Pictures are very important at the time of the renter's decision!

5. And do not forget, the more information you make available, the more chances you'll have to close a good deal!

By the way, it will be great if you already know about real estate insurance. If not, then do read up.

CHAPTER 25
VACATION PROPERTY BROKER

Here's a bit of history to consider. Less than 20 years ago, brokers only relied on the phone, shoe sole, and newspaper ads to capture clients and real estate. Presentations, tables and simulations of proposals were delivered on paper only, in person or via mail. The most ease one had was being able to use the old fax machine to send some document. Fortunately, this reality has changed radically, and all needs of customer service have come to rely on technological resources, which were further favored by the popularization of social networks and the possibility of access to information from mobile devices.

With this, today, as in any segment, the real estate market and the internet have become inseparable. And so has the role of a vacation property broker changed drastically.

And as I have mentioned above for various roles, mentioning a few tips here to make the best use of this relationship and be a successful vacation property broker.

1 - GAIN KNOWLEDGE
Make no mistake that knowledge is a solid foundation for success to be achieved. In fact, you may even be a good

connoisseur of the various features that the internet is able to offer. But do you know all the tools so well that you know how to exploit them to the fullest?

Therefore, look for courses and training aimed at the techniques of using the tools that the internet offers.

2 - SEGMENT YOUR TARGET AUDIENCE

The possibilities of the internet are unlimited. However, in such a large and comprehensive universe, if you do not create specific foci, and especially in the sector of vacation properties, you may get very limited results if they arise. Therefore, it is critical that you map out the profiles of the types of audiences you want to meet and design your other actions accordingly. For example, differentiate your actions and campaigns between people who want to rent for shorter intervals, and those who want to rent it for longer intervals.

3 - CREATE A PAGE ON FACEBOOK AND RELEASE IT

It is not unusual for the broker to have a personal profile on Facebook and, through it, among the photos of the weekend, publishes real estate offers or needs funding. If you act like this, among the friends of the network, eventually you may even find who is buying or selling a property, which does not invalidate the whole initiative. However, you will find much greater success if you professionalize your presence on Facebook. To do so, start by creating a page where only information and images related to your real estate business will be published. To get started, invite your Facebook friends to enjoy the page, but do not be alone in it. After all, 1,000 or 2,000 users represent success in promoting the page to your direct audience, but it does not represent that you will succeed in business.

So, invest in the promotion of the page, seeking users and potential renters beyond your audience. Make this investment rationally by setting a budget that is compatible with your ability to pay and distribute the promotion amount very carefully.

4 - INVEST IN THE DISCLOSURE OF THE OFFERS AND THE DEMANDS

Part of that budget of disclosure of the page or an exclusive amount you must reserve to promote specific offers and demands pertaining to the seasonal nature of the property, for example (off-seasons and on-seasons).

5 - CREATE A WEBSITE

Today's websites are fundamental for someone to be present on the internet consistently. In it, you can not only present your offers and demands but also outline your areas of expertise and professional experience, as well as create a channel of contact with potential buyers and sellers. However, since the first impression is the one that stays, take care to register an easily assimilated domain and to have the site professionally prepared.

Do not forget to integrate your site with Facebook and other social networks, and also take care that it is responsive in order to become visible from all operating systems, considering that today most of the internet access is done through of mobile devices.

6 - HAVE AN EMAIL ACCOUNT WITH THE EXTENSION OF YOUR SITE

Really, it is quite practical to use the free email accounts of Google, Yahoo or Outlook. You can also use a real estate account to which you may be associated. However, considering that you have invested in creating a website, which requires a domain of your own, having an email account of the type "yourname@yourdomain.com" will certainly create a more professional and credible image that will be very favorable to your performance to the clientele.

7 - INVEST IN GOOGLE ADWORDS

Investing in Google Adwords greatly improves the visibility of your site, which can appear in ads on other sites. Include that investment in your total budget, which is relatively cheaper than the forms of marketing and advertising of traditional campaigns. In addition, from this strategy, you can target the audience you want to reach.

8 - CREATE A CHANNEL ON YOUTUBE

A survey by Ibope found that 64% of people looking for real estate access YouTube for information. This number makes it very interesting to maintain a channel on the site, where you can display videos of your offers and the differences with regards to parameters and changes which keep happening to the property. Eventually, if you are a good communicator, you can even produce videos with different information about the real estate market, which will be useful for generating access and attracting customers.

SECTION

THREE

LEARNING SKILL BASED METHODS TO EARN PASSIVE INCOME

CHAPTER 26
STANDARD RATE AND DATA SERVICE
(SRDS)

Today, a lot is said about performance, scalability, process automation, and business productivity issues. For those who live the day to day life of a CIO in large companies, or closely follow what happens in the IT areas of these companies, this becomes even more evident. We are becoming increasingly concerned about what needs to be done to reduce accounts and increase performance. Delivering results faster by spending less, without hampering processes, increasing productivity whenever possible, is a constant goal.

To meet the new demands more quickly, the tools and services related to cloud computing have been gaining evidence and relevance over time. A good example of this is the Software as a Service (SaaS) concept. Since the arrival of solutions based on this concept, many attitudes in IT management began to be questioned, which paved the way for its constant evolution.

SaaS consists of providing one or more software typically over the Internet in the service model, usually paid monthly, and its cost can vary by several factors, such as number of users, resources used, among others. See below for the best benefits that SaaS usage can add to you and your team:

1. REDUCING LICENSE COSTS

Because they are almost always based on periodic payments, the high cost for software licenses is set aside. These monthly payments (also with other options such as quarterly, half-yearly and yearly payments) are more accessible than the old licenses for product versions, as well as allowing better control over the long term, without any surprises in financial planning.

2. REDUCING INFRASTRUCTURE AND MAINTENANCE

Because they are hosted in the cloud publicly or privately to your company, using SaaS enables you to reduce your infrastructure to the fullest. More servers are taking up space, consuming energy, demanding hours of maintenance and care from your IT staff.

3. FOCUS ON YOUR BUSINESS

When choosing a service, you do not have to worry so much about your internal infrastructure, periodic and emergency maintenance, backups of your data, and manual software upgrades when using SaaS. You and your entire team gain more time to focus on the daily work and knowledge in the evolution of your own business.

4. GREAT PARTNER OF TI BIMODAL

TI Bimodal is a rapidly growing trend, as it allows the union of two IT models to achieve more agility and innovation without leaving aside the solidity and responsible evolution within the business environment.

5. DATA SECURITY AND AVAILABILITY ASSURANCES

When adopting a SaaS, you should be aware that a lot of your company information is going to a server in the cloud, such as communication, tasks, plans, projects, and so on. But whenever the doubts come up and make you question the whole process, remember all the work you and your team had to perform and maintain backups of your entire structure, without error-freeness and setbacks. Now think that this is the responsibility of the provider of that service.

6. ACCESS ANYTIME, ANYWHERE

One of the basic principles of SaaS is that it is accessible anytime, anywhere. Through a browser and an internet connection, its users have easy access at any time, making it an important differential that allows more mobility, agility and practicality for all employees inside and outside the business environment.

7. CONSTANT UPDATES

Your system update issues end here. No worries about operating system versions and minimum workstation requirements so that new versions of your software can be installed and working properly. In SaaS, the update in question happens on the provider side, and you do not have to worry - no downloads of endless patches and time-consuming installations.

Following this list of advantages, we can safely say that SaaS has come to stay in the IT market.

CHAPTER 27
WRITER (GHOSTWRITING)

If you love working with words, then one of the ways on how to make money on the internet is by becoming a freelance copywriter. Even if you do not have experience in this activity, you can start without major problems. And already get to get some money from it. The first thing you need to think about is a niche and decide what type of writing you will use. For example:

There are a bunch of contents, almost infinite, which you can write and specialize. Your main decision will be what kind of writer you will be and exactly what you are going to work with. Once you've decided, it's time to start creating some samples of your work and spreading them over the net. Some of the most popular channels for doing this are LinkedIn and Medium. Both platforms are great places to show your full potential.

If you are already starting to get started, we recommend some content with extra tips on what you can do as a freelance writer.

CHAPTER 28
TRANSLATION SERVICE
(BACKSEAT TRANSLATOR)

This profile is pretty self-explanatory in terms of the roles and responsibilities one would have to undertake if trying this. I think the more important and more necessary thing is to actually understand the environment the freelance translator will find in the current translation market.

This will also be useful to prepare an efficient business plan since, as in any type of business, planning must always be the first step for those who start some economic activity. Therefore, the topics discussed below will help demystify, un-complicate and broaden the view on the positioning of the translation business for freelancers in the market.

To begin with, I must make it clear that the translation service should only be done by people who completely dominate two or more languages. This is also a complex activity because translators should learn to deal with situations that make service delivery even more difficult. Among the situations that the freelancer translator will find are problems with source text and language problems. The most frequent problems with the source text are incomplete texts, non-digitized texts, poorly printed texts, poorly scanned texts, Poorly written texts, lack of references, quotes without the original text, changes in the text during the translation process.

Already with the language, you can come across the following situations: language too technical, literary texts written in a very old language, texts with strong regionalist influences, dialects, unexplained abbreviations, own names, names of organizations, slang and jargon, idiomatic expressions, redundant phrases, language conventions and agreements and graphical accentuations.

Any of these situations, if not very well observed, organized and adapted by the translator, could interfere in the target language and the interpretation that the readers will have of the message of the translated text.

Another highlight among the language problems most faced by translators euphonic and dissonance, cultural characteristics, poetic texts, puns, specific idiomatic properties, rhymes, common terms in one region but unknown in another (for these cases it is necessary a clear explanation of what one wants to convey), and false cognates, which are similar words in two languages, but which have the different meaning, for example: the word "scene." In Portuguese, it is a reference to the space occupied by the stage of a theatre; In Spanish, it means "dinner."

TRANSLATION AS A PROFESSION

There is no need for proof to certify the translator's ability. But of course, the market is not silly and will always select the best prepared to meet your needs. The lack of regulation, in general, makes it easier for freelancers to access the market, who only need to master their native language very well and at least have an intermediate / advanced level in the foreign language.

THE PROFILE OF THE TRANSLATOR IN THE RECENT HISTORY

But to understand the role of translation with a more modern view, we will have to focus on the recent history of the profession and retreat only seven or eight decades ago. In this way, we will be able to understand how the freelancers' routine in the translation market was in the early 20th century.

At that time, for example, a translator of scientific literature was probably a teacher or scientist, almost always retired, who had vast knowledge in its area of expertise. Only the experience of having worked and studied his whole life on a particular branch was already the guarantee that his translation would be faithful and reliable. In this case, the translator was something like a traveling library that, in addition to its native language, dominated one or more foreign languages. If we consider that at that time there were not many language schools, nor computers, let alone translation tools like Google Translator, we will conclude that being a translator meant to belong to a profession of the highest level, restricted to a select group of professionals specialized and experienced, who translated specific texts, being limited only to their areas of activity. For example, only a doctor could translate a text about medicine; or, only a philosopher would faithfully translate a text of philosophy.

Nowadays, anyone with a computer that is curious and who likes to research can be a translator, achieving levels of fidelity and reliability of translation equal to and even superior to those pioneers of the beginning of the last century. The great advantages of modern translators are: the ease of access to infinite information, through literature and the Internet; intensive language courses, increasingly fast and of acceptable quality; computers and translation software that streamline and facilitate the process; and online communities of freelance translators who help each other, solving each other's doubts and difficulties.

Today, virtually anyone with an acceptable domain of at least two languages can translate any type of text, even without ever having contact with a specific area of the market.

THE TRANSLATION MARKET

I will conclude with some basic information on the translation market, under the following aspects: Literary, technical, media and journalistic translations so that you get the basic idea of how translations work in these verticals.

LITERARY TRANSLATION

Foreign authors, once unknown, are successful and stick their titles among the world bestsellers. Result: there is a growing need to translate these titles into several languages around the globe. One of the great examples of this is the abysmal number of books put up for sale without any mediation from the former publishers. There have been cases of authors, almost anonymous, and ignored by large publishers, who make thousands of dollars monthly by selling their books and e-books on retail Internet sites like Amazon.com, for example.

TECHNICAL

Technical translation currently accounts for approximately 90% of translations. Usually, they are manuals of products and machines; texts related to medicine; administration, economics and finance; electronics or mechanics in general.

MEDIA TRANSLATION

It has to do with subtitling of audio and video. Just to give an example, it is known that this is a shortage in the market, due to the lack of specific courses and training.

TRANSLATION JOURNALISM

Again, globalization. In this case, and in general, it is the journalists themselves who carry out the translations, adapting the world news to the local language.

CHAPTER 29
FREELANCING

Let's face it, starting your own agency is a little intimidating, and not everyone is confident to do it straight away. Once you have your own team of highly skilled professionals put together, you may want to try out something that does not involve that much of a risk and will still get you paid. Thankfully, there are tons of freelancing websites like Upwork out there that allow you to sell your skills to potential business owners for a fair price.

There are a lot of benefits to working on these websites, and one of them is that you have a minimum investment in terms of space. You can also learn from your mistakes that you make as a freelancer and use those lessons for when you start planning your own agency. Freelancing is great because it gives you the opportunity to work with people all across the globe, and this helps you to understand market trends everywhere. The more time you spend freelancing, the stronger your profile gets, and this makes it easier for you to start your business with confidence.

At the end of the day, your main goal is to establish your own social media marketing agency, so whichever way you get there, it is always going to be something that you want to achieve. The reason it makes more sense for you to practice before you actually take the plunge is that this helps you to recognize what your weak points are and it helps you to work on them before you actually start investing money in the business and then try to rectify the problem.

SECTION

FOUR

LEARNING OFFLINE METHODS TO EARN PASSIVE INCOME

CHAPTER 30
PHOTOGRAPHY ROYALTY
(STOCK PHOTOGRAPHER)

T he search for how to make money with photography grows with each passing day. Making money with photography can be the perfect work option, with no fixed schedule and high profitability, of course, for this you need to learn how to make money with photography, from the option clichés like weddings, birthdays and graduations to the sale of images on the Internet.

Currently, the list of possibilities to make money with photography is great, and the investment is affordable, so if you are looking for how to make money with photography, this content is perfect! I've done a search and reviewed the most promising ways and ideas to make money with photography

ANIMAL PHOTOGRAPHY

The pet sector has been growing for years, in 2018 the percentage was 9%. If you want to learn how to make money with photography and have ease with pets here is an excellent option to make money with photos. The focus should be on investing in good scenarios and characterizing pets, like the work of photographing babies. To start in this niche and to make money with photography the investment is very accessible, basically the professional equipment of photographers, scenarios and some clothes for the animals.

MAKE MONEY WITH PHOTOGRAPHY IN EVENTS

Events such as weddings, graduations, birthdays, and parties, in general, can be highly lucrative for photographers. The problem faced is a large number of professionals and mainly companies responsible for organizing the entire event, consequently providing their own photographers. The good news is that it is an option to make money with highly profitable photography, perhaps the highest paid, and you can charge values over R $ 1,000 per event.

BABY PHOTOGRAPHY

Babies are the perfect audience for those who want to make money with photography and at the same time spend little and have a loyal clientele. The photos start already in the first months, and every year the parents come back, again, to the photographer to take photos. Normally, photographs of babies remain until the age of 4, maintaining a good stabilization of clients.

Just like in photographs of pets, this case requires nice scenery, toys, and different outfits to make the babies even cuter and would guarantee an eternal memory for their parents. The marketing of the work is fundamental to make money with photographing babies, and a good form of publicity is the use of social networks like Instagram and Facebook, which are cheap, allow information sharing and are frequently accessed by the parents.

PHOTOS FOR E-COMMERCE SITES AND OTHER SITES

E-commerce websites need high-resolution, quality photos that interpret the context. For example, the images of products sold to the store should arouse the visitor's buying interest, so its importance. Studies already indicate that images in the products offered significantly increase the purchase rate, especially when they are of good quality.

CREATING A FASHION BLOG OR PHOTOGRAPHY

The photography professional can work with digital marketing and have their own business. Blogs of photography and fashion, for example, usually have many accesses and with that, it is possible to monetize.

PHOTO SERVICES WITH DRONES

The use of Drones is on the rise in many professions. In photography and video recording, you can get excellent results from images, provided you have quality equipment.

Aerial event photography is one of the people's favorite requests for photographers, and many are failing to take advantage of this opportunity. Invest now in a drone and equipment to shoot and record videos, it will surely be a differential in your profession, and you can increase your income with photography.

SALE OF PHOTOS - STOCK PHOTOS

Do you like to take photos professionally and have creativity? Did you know that there are sites where images can be made available for sale in a simple, practical and highly profitable way? Also known as a Stock photographer, it is one that assembles a vast repertoire of images and makes them available in marketplaces, that is, platforms of sale of images.

In these platforms, the interested ones pay the value by the image and use, avoiding complications with copyrights. Good examples of marketplaces to sell the photographs are Photodune, Fotolia, Bigstock and Shutterstock.

CHAPTER 31
DIVIDEND INCOME
(DIVIDEND-PAYING STOCKS)

Many investors say this a lot of times, "I have R $ X.000, is it a good idea to invest in the stock market?"

The first thing you should know is yes; it is possible to make money on the stock exchange. This market offers many earning opportunities, with several examples of success, such as those achieved by fund managers. Managers who have profited more than 30% in the last 24 months - which is a much better performance than savings and much higher than the Ibovespa, lost -2% in the same period.

In times of markets in crisis, stop and think: how much was your profitability in the last 12 months? Did you earn $ 200 for every $ 1000 invested? It's not that easy. The stock exchange is not that easy. Many investors are tempted to "make a fortune in the stock market," start investing on their own, do not know enough and end up coming out worse than they entered.

An alternative that I recommend is not going into the stock market alone. Instead, invest through an investment fund that has behind it a professional manager who will study the market and invest your money for you.

Hire a Professional. Unlike many investors imagine, having a professional manager looking after your money is very easy, simple and cheap, in addition to being more profitable most of the time.

Managers have access to information that the investor alone does not have. They use modern analysis and simulation tools, as well as having a team 100% focused on the search for the best opportunities in the market. "But I have a profit by investing alone!" Many investors go so far as to delude themselves that the only thing that matters is having a positive profitability. In fact, the important thing is to compare your profitability with the market as a whole. What I mean is that it's no use thinking you're a great investor if you've earned 10% in the year, while the market has risen by 15%.

I also want to use this opportunity to tell you about the advantages of a professional manager. He offers several advantages compared to venturing alone on the stock exchange.

1. CLEAR OBJECTIVE
The manager already has the pre-determined rules about what the fund can and cannot do, ensuring much more security for investors who apply money.

2. OPPORTUNISTIC AND DYNAMIC STRATEGY

This is the main highlight and difference of the fund compared to other products on the market. Through a dynamic and opportunistic strategy, the professional managers (example: JGP Equity Works) operate by buying and selling according to market movements. With this agility, they are able to take advantage of the best opportunities of the moment and have great capacity of protection of capital in low moments.

3. WELL-DEFINED RISK RULES

The investment fund has clear risk exposure criteria; it ensures that the manager does not take more risk than it should. This is very rare among individual investors since it is often quite complicated to calculate and determine the risk of a particular transaction.

4. 100% FOCUSED ON STOCKS

This condition guarantees that the fund manager will always be attentive to the stock exchange, seeking to determine what the best actions for each moment are.

CHAPTER 32
COMMODITIES TRADING

Binary Trading continues to grow in popularity as the industry has witnessed an increase in the number of traders each year. However, traders have to rely on a certain level of skill to be successful in trading binary options. Your success depends on choosing the right assets to trade, deciding how much to invest, determining the periods you want to use for analysis, and in what direction they want to bet.

If you are a beginner trader in binary options and want to be successful at it, then you need to realize that there is a lot to learn. One of the most important things you should keep in mind as a beginner trader is that you should be very patient and use a strategic approach if you are looking to earn profits consistently in your trading of binary options. You should not let your emotions keep you from giving your best, and you should not stray from your trading strategy.

Binary options traders do not need to buy the actual asset. Let's look at a typical example of binary trading. Suppose you decide to create trading based on the future value of gold, where you need to determine if the price of gold will fall or rise during a stipulated period. You do not have to buy any gold bar for this transaction, because the only thing you need is to put money in your forecast and wait for the results.

Because binary options are extremely simple to understand and negotiate, they soon have become one of the most popular platforms when it comes to financial trading. These options trades give traders the opportunity to make quick gains that are determined by the type of asset you choose and by choosing the direction in trading binary options. To make a profit using binary options, it all boils down to correctly determining the price movement of a given market or asset over a stipulated time.

One of the main differences when it comes to traditional trading and binary options trading is that a trader will lose 100% of his investment if he misses the prognosis in binary trading, while he will probably withhold some of his investment when trading in the traditional market, although the asset acquired may have depreciated significantly.

If you want to be successful in trading binary options, it is important that you take the time to educate yourself about trading binary options before you get seriously involved. We have already made it clear that trading binary options involve speculating on the value of a particular asset over a stipulated time. When a trader decides that the underlying asset is going to go up, he goes ahead and buys an 'UP' option. If the trader believes that the underlying asset will fall, he will buy a 'DOWN' option.

For the trader to make money from the 'UP' transaction, the price of the underlying asset must exceed the strike price by the due date. For the trader to make money with the 'DOWN', then the price of the underlying asset should be lower than the strike price by the due date. The strike price, also known as the strike price, is determined by the value level of the underlying asset when the trader buys the binary option. The trader will be able to find out the strike price, expiration date, risk, and payment before entering the transaction.

After the transaction is completed, trading is started and there is nothing else the trader can do except wait for the expiration of the term and then see the end result.

WHAT ARE BINARY OPTIONS STRATEGIES?

These are the broad strategies which one needs to keep in mind:

1. TREND CAPTURE

When the term 'trend capture' is used in the context of binary options, it is important to note that it is not being used to pinpoint trends that last the last two weeks or months but is highlighting mini-trends that have occurred in the hours or minutes. If you want to be a successful binary options trader, careful monitoring of breaking news is critical so you can take advantage of these trends and become successful in trading binary options.

2. REVERSION STRATEGY

Binary options traders have the option of combining the above trend capture strategy with the reversal strategy we will explain below. To implement the two strategies together, it will be necessary for the trader to have a certain amount of technical know-how to succeed with this dual strategy. All trends tend to reverse over time. Traders who are well versed in the industry can use charts to determine with a certain level of accuracy when a trend is about to reverse. They can profit from this trend when it begins a reversal of direction and reverse.

WHAT ARE THE BENEFITS?

There are a number of benefits in investing in binary options when compared to investing in more traditional trading methods.

SPEED

Investors who follow the traditional trading market route realize that it can take weeks, months and even years before they make any profit from their investment. However, trading binary options gives traders quicker results, although there are some binary options that allow traders to trade on a long-term basis.

POTENTIAL PROFITS & RETURNS

Unlike traditional investments, binary options give traders the opportunity to make potential profits of up to 80% while trading in the short term. Although the return on investment is extremely high, it is important to note that it is also extremely risky. If an investor invests $ 100 in a short-term binary options deal and hits, he may receive an additional $ 80. However, if he makes a mistake, he may end up losing his $ 100.

GLOBAL MARKET ACCESS

Binary options traders have access to global markets and the opportunity to choose from hundreds of underlying stock-market assets around the world.

GETTING PROFITS FROM UP AND DOWN MARKETS

One of the great advantages of trading binary options is that traders can make money regardless of current market conditions as they have the option of selecting stocks when the market is going up, down or even walking laterally.

You can read at greater lengths about trading from a number of sources, but what is more important according to me, are the tips mentioned below:

SELECT A GOOD BINARY OPTIONS BROKER

The most important advice any binary options trader needs is to make sure you have chosen the correct binary options broker when you begin. A good broker with a solid reputation in the market will know how to do your job and can make all the difference in the way you perform with your trading of binary options.

DIVERSIFY YOUR TRADING

The number of online binary options brokers has grown significantly in recent years, thanks to the increase in the number of binary options traders. While this gives binary option traders a wide range of options when it comes to selecting the binary options broker, it can also be a tricky task as it can be difficult to decide which brokerage is right for you.

ENJOY THE BONUSES

When you are starting with trading binary options, you should make the most of the number of sign-up bonuses that are offered to new traders. These bonuses are provided in an effort to get new binary option traders and are credited to the trader's account after the completion of the registration process. Traders can use these special bonuses as a protection against their real money traders, and to increase their chances of making a profit on their first trading.

EARLY RELEASE NEGOTIATIONS

When you start trading with binary options, you will find that sometimes you will have an option known as an early exit option in some of your dealings. This is a very complicated offer because you can eliminate the risk by going out early, but on the other hand, if you stay, there is a possibility that your transaction will perform better if you stay through the entire previous trading period. If you decide to take the early exit option, you will earn a lower profit, not the full amount you were guaranteed within the stipulated trading period.

AVOID TIPS AND RUMORS

As you continue to trade with binary options, you will find a lot of information on your way, offering you a wide range of tips and assertions that will give you a so-called advantage when it comes to trading options. Keep in mind that when it comes to trading binary options, there is no guarantee that any strategy will work all the time. Your best bet is to invest time to do an in-depth market analysis and then make a decision based on the information you have researched and bet on a negotiation. This is the best way to increase the likelihood of you profiting from trading binary options.

On top of all this, to be a successful professional in binary options, it is critical that you control your emotions. You need to be able to manage your ups and downs, and not negotiate when you feel emotionally disturbed as this will likely have a negative impact on your trading.

HOW MUCH MONEY CAN YOU EARN THROUGH BINARY OPTIONS TRADING

While most financial products tend to be a bit too complicated for the average person, binary options are based on a yes / no decision, making it one of the financial products simpler to negotiate. Dealers can get between 70% and 90% of their trading profits, depending on the online binary options trading platform they choose, the assets they select, and the time frames they choose. Most binary options traders prefer to choose an online binary options trading platform that allows them to bet on trades that have a very short expiration period. This allows these traders to cash in on their transactions within minutes. Although it sounds too good to be true, it is important for traders to understand that there is a mathematical composition associated with trading binary options and it becomes easier for a trader to be consistently successful when he understands how this mathematical composition operates.

The main formula of these compound returns is to constantly increase the profits of the transactions while the binary options are negotiated. The easiest way to explain this is to use an example. Let's assume you make a $ 2000 deposit into your account and then use 5% of that balance to open a deal on your binary options trading platform, where the profit is 70%. If your forecast is correct and you make a profit from trading, your payment will be $ 170;

where $ 100 is your bet money and $ 70 is your profit. Once the composite return principle applies, the trader will have to invest the full amount, that is, $ 170 in his next trading and if he finishes hitting again, he will receive $ 289.

CHAPTER 33
FOREIGN LANGUAGE BUSINESS

E very parent knows the importance of mastering foreign languages for the future of their child. Due to this fact, many parents have already thought about the case or have already put their children into language courses. Nowadays, there is still one more facility: the partnerships between language schools/individuals and educational institutions.

HOW IT WORKS
Partnerships between language schools/individuals and educational institutions can start with the interest of the educational institution or language schools / individuals. Working together, their teachers, coordinators, principals, and other academic members set up a contract, think through methodologies, adapt their own school environment, and more to better language learning.

But the courses taught by their language counterpart do not work like any class. Firstly, you should do the leveling of the students, which will define their class (as if it were in normal formation, in which age does not define its class, but it's level in the defined language).

The methodology is also a bit different, such as lessons to learn pronunciation by audio or movies. This cooperation between the traditional school and the language course has many benefits.

BENEFITS FOR PARENTS

This partnership provides your child with greater security and comfort, since lessons can be taught in the school's own environment. The child having language classes in the school itself also allows a greater saving in extra expenses, such as the transportation used to follow up course, for example.

BENEFITS FOR THE CHILDREN

Your child will efficiently learn the chosen language, one of the most basic benefits. There is also greater ease with foreign language classes per se, because of the already familiar school environment, which gives your child greater confidence (he feels less embarrassed, for example, being able to develop further).

WHAT THE EDUCATIONAL INSTITUTION IMPROVES

With an increasingly competitive education-related market, having a prominent differential can make the school stand out. Providing parents with a monthly fee for cheaper courses and ensuring the safety of the child is certainly a great attraction for new students.

WHAT GAIN IN PARTNERSHIPS BETWEEN LANGUAGE SCHOOLS AND INSTITUTIONS

Bringing language courses to an educational institution will attract new students accurately. Be it for the monthly tuition discounts, or for the greater security of the parents (who did not want their children to travel the school-course, for example) and more. And the students in the partnership classes can indicate the language school for acquaintances, which attracts even more students.

Given all these benefits, it is possible to understand why the partnership between educational institutions and a language school can be so rewarding. It is almost like a guarantee of a successful income generating service, which is making and filling an important gap in the education sector.

CHAPTER 34
CAR RENTAL

This is another one of those profiles where I would like to explain the need which exists in the current society for car rentals and why the number of people opting for it will keep on increasing continuously. Currently, having a new car in the garage is not necessarily just a matter of hobby or vanity. In fact, the car, much more than a simple vehicle of locomotion, has become an alternative for those who want to increase their monthly income. But is the best way to enjoy the benefits of owning a new car is by getting one? Or is it more advantageous to ride with a zero car, hiring a car rental plan?

Lately, much has been discussed about the advantages or disadvantages of having a car by subscription, a service that is being made available by the rental companies and that, little by little, is gaining strength in the country. In order for you to draw your own conclusions, I am going to bring to you the possible benefits or losses in choosing to buy a new vehicle or joining the vehicle subscription service.

Most of the vehicles on the streets are in service. The tendency to turn the car into an extra source of income is getting stronger among people. This is easily proven if we consider that most of the vehicles on the streets are in the service of applications, such as Uber, among others. One of the great balconies of this type of transport is that, when calling the driver, it is necessary to inform the origin and destination addresses of the trip.

The convenience of being able to drink in the ballad and not having to worry about driving on the way back home also makes the car application service very much in demand. And for the driver too, there are many advantages! The possibility of it deciding how much money you want to earn, since the more customers you get, the more profitable the business is, it's a big draw, for example. That is, the driver is the one who makes the profit itself!

And the value of all the trips of the week that the app driver performs will be deposited into your checking account or savings on a single weekly deposit. With all these advantages, for drivers and users, and the consequent adherence of people to transportation applications, you may be thinking that the demand for vehicles has decreased, have not you?

The flexibility in the use of the vehicle influences the demand for vehicles in the automotive market. Contrary to what one might imagine, the demand for cars in the country did not decline with the emergence of the new mode of transportation by application. Research has pointed to a considerable increase in demand for new cars in recent years. The flexibility in the use of the vehicle, therefore, directly influences the growth of the demand for vehicles in the automotive market. That is, there is a greater number of people using vehicles, either to move with more agility and safety or for comfort or work.

WHAT DOES ONE MEAN BY OWNING A CAR BY SIGNATURE?

The pay-per-car service consists of offering monthly or annual car rental plans.

Already very common in the United States and Europe, the option to hire a service of signing new cars is also becoming an accessible reality in the market. The service consists of offering monthly or annual car rental plans. These plans are offered by insurers, rental companies and even by mobile applications. That way, you can ride with zero worries about financing or any other way of acquiring the vehicle. You also will not need to stress about the payment of insurance, IPVA, licensing, or even periodic reviews and maintenance of the property.

In addition, it is possible for the user to leave the car at the time of signing the contract. This is very important since some people need to use the car on the same day as the agreement.

To make it cheaper for a car by subscription, it is possible that more people from the same family use the vehicle, which is a" hand in the wheel."

However, as this type of service is new in the market, it is necessary that we make a deeper assessment, because it is fundamental, for those who work with the car and take their livelihood, knowing which of the options to maintain a vehicle is the most profitable. With that in mind, I will compare the advantages of owning a new car by subscription and purchasing a new car through financing (the vehicle's most common vehicle acquisition mode in the country).

The fact that the user of the vehicle does not have to worry about the rush and the expenses related to the payment of taxes is already quite attractive! As we have seen above, the car service subscription offers numerous user facilities.

For example, the fact that the user of the vehicle does not need to worry about the rush and the expenses related to the payment of taxes (IPVA, Licensing) is an attractive and so much, right? Another advantage is that the maintenance and the necessary revisions to the good functioning of the vehicle are all on account of the company that provides the car, that is, the user is also free of the concern with these values. In addition, the instructor says that you do not need to stress about the maintenance of the car, because it is attended with agility anywhere. And finally, another attractive feature of car subscription service is the ease of leasing.

CHAPTER 35
RENT YOUR CAR FOR AD SPACE

Have you ever thought about turning your car costs into profit without making any extra effort? With platforms like Carlicity, this is possible, and - to earn extra money - you simply follow your routine as usual. These are a meeting platform for advertising cars with their advertisers. This means that you register your vehicle and inform your normal routine, and the platform selects some advertisers that fit your offer.

If you accept any of these offers, your car will be affixed, and you will receive money monthly, according to the signed contract. There is no cost to the owner of the car, and just drive normally on the itinerary indicated.

To participate, you simply register on the platform, register the car you have, with the brand, model, year, color, and the itinerary you usually do, as well as your schedules. Whenever you find a demand that complies with your routine, the platforms will advise you, telling you what the monthly offer paid by the advertiser company is. If you agree, the advertiser company is responsible for all the costs of bonding and care, and you only need to direct and receive the money at the end of the month. If you do not want to promote that ad, just decline the offer and wait for the next one.

HOW MUCH DO I GET WITH THE STICKER?

The amount you receive depends, of course, on the city, the type of advertisement, the type of car, and the itinerary that you travel through. In general, the factor that most influences the value received is the path travelled. That means that the more miles traveled daily, the higher the amount received at the end of the month, according to the combined service across the platform. In addition, various companies include special contract offers such as fuel supply, recurring washes, or other advantages that are interesting to both the driver and the advertiser.

FINAL
WORDS

I hope you enjoyed checking out the various methods you can earn good money through passive income! While this may all seem very lucrative and interesting, it's essential you find your calling and stick to something you know will work well for you. Trial and error is part of the game, but make sure you experiment with the ones you're passionate about!

Finally, if you found this book useful in any way, a review on Amazon is always appreciated!

Jonathan Fitzpatrick

SIGN UP!

Visit our website
WWW.JONATHANFITZPATRICKAUTHOR.COM
and enter your email address to receive exclusive
bonus contents related to the updates of this book
and find out all about Jonathan Fitzpatrick's new
publications, launch offers and other exclusive
promotions!

JONATHAN
FITZPATRICK

JONATHAN FITZPATRICK'S
OTHER PUBLICATIONS

available at
amazon

AMAZON FBA MASTERY COACHING

THE DEFINITIVE GUIDE TO LEARN THE SECRET WAY TO SELL FULFILLMENT BY AMAZON

HOW TO LAUNCH A PRIVATE LABEL AND EARN SIX FIGURES OF PASSIVE INCOME IN AN EASY STEP-BY-STEP METHOD FROM TOTAL BEGINNERS TO REALLY ADVANCED

What is Amazon FBA? What can I do with FBA? Is it as challenging as my colleagues at work keep saying? Is it worth the trouble? Depending on how well you know or understand Fulfillment By Amazon, these are some of the questions you may have asked yourself. Well, look no further because this book is the ultimate compass t making money, and possibly a lot of it, online through FBA.

It matters not where at what point this book finds you. If you have made the conscious decision to see positive change in life, then with this book there is no looking back. Take a deep breath and believe that the transformation is already set in motion. Frankly speaking, if you are already this far, the ball is definitely already rolling. For what it is worth, I do believe in you.

Inside you will find valuable, and quite possibly life-saving, information designed to let you first understand the basic principles of the journey you are embarking on. You will learn what essentially is the premise of human psychology and the dark approach to it as well. Furthermore, you will delve into in depth summation of the techniques. With each technique is a concise elaboration of the approach and impact. At your beck and call, you will have a priceless treasure that is meant to propel you to gaining insight into the hidden secrets of the psychological world.

You being here has unequivocally taken a lot of gut and conviction. The biggest hurdle is ever getting started and it is the stumbling block for many individuals. Boldly take that first step. Do not let yourself get complacent. Get started by buying this book today!

Inside you will find:

The blueprint to building an FBA business and empire.

Guidelines on how to get started with Amazon FBA in 2020.

Guidelines on products, listing, and shipping.

 Gaining traction and feedback on your products.

Strategies and techniques for gaining an advantage over your competitors.

And more…

available at

RENTAL PROPERTY INVESTING

SECRETS OF A REAL ESTATE BUILDING EMPIRE

available at
amazon

PRINCIPLES TO MAKE 7 FIGURES OF A PASSIVE INCOME ESTABLISHING A REAL ESTATE INVESTMENT EMPIRE

You are looking for something. Something is out there waiting for you, you just know it. It is your salvation, your saving grace, the path to the lifestyle you have always known you were born to live. The question is: what is IT?

IT is real estate rental property and it is the key to your future as a smart business owner who knows what they want and goes out to get it. It is the excitement of finding the perfect rental property for the perfect tenant and bringing in the cash to find the next perfect property and begin all over again. And this book, *Rental Property Investing: Secrets of a Real Estate Building Empire: Principles to Make 7 Figures of a Passive Income Establishing a Real Estate Investment Empire* is the book that holds the keys to your future. When you follow the steps outlined in this book you will become the real estate rental property investor that you always wanted to be, on your way to living the life you always knew you were meant to live.

You will learn why real estate is the perfect career for anyone who has the passion to be successful at it. You will learn how to locate good properties for rental properties and exactly the steps you need to take to purchase them. You will see the difference between different types of properties and how each one can make you a successful entrepreneur.

We will show you who you need to surround yourself with to make yourself successful. We will discuss ways to buy property when you really don't have the money to spare. And we will discuss whether or not flipping is the way for you to acquire your new rental properties.

Investing in real estate rental property seems scary because buying a house is a big purchase and most people only buy one or two at a time. You want to buy dozens. But this book will show you how it is done and why you don't need to fear the future in your new career. You were meant to do this; you just need to begin.

Above all everything you need to know is explained in words you can understand, with examples where needed. And all the tips and tricks you will need to become successful is right here in this book. This is the book that will lead you to the beginning of your new career, one that will get you to the path take you through the rest of your life.

available at

PASSIVE INCOME

THE HOLY GRAIL OF FINANCIAL FREEDOM

available at
amazon

THE SIDE HUSTLE BLUEPRINT TO LEARN HOW TO MAKE MONEY WITHOUT BEING ACTIVELY INVOLVED

You have a regular 9 to 5 job and every month you receive a salary that pays the bills, but in the back of your mind, you have that will to gain a little more. You may want to have a little more freedom to work as you want to, from where you want. Until one fine day, you finally decide to change that reality and put your dreams first. Sounds familiar? Great! In this scenario, the best thing is to invest in any kind of activity that can generate passive income.

This book is the best way for you to learn more about passive income and how it can give you the freedom that you desire. This book will give you all the information you need regarding passive income and how you can go about learning the various techniques. These techniques have been tried and tested by successful entrepreneurs across the world, and you will love the ideas that you will read here. But before you move forward, you need to know what passive income is all about.

What is Passive Income?

Passive income is earned from an activity or an occupation that does not demand continuous "active" work and is still capable of generating income. Passive income activities usually involve a lot of work during the creation process - but once finalized and launched, these activities can generate steady profits for a long time.

A classic example is an online course. You will spend a few weeks or even months creating the site and the material. Then you will not have to work that hard anymore, and you will continue to make a profit. The same goes for a virtual store, with videos and even with books.

With passive income, it is possible to generate money even without working every day - and that is why so many entrepreneurs want to know more about the subject.

With this book, you will learn all the techniques that you need to generate a six-figure income without too much effort from your end. All you need to do is sit back and enjoy your financial freedom.

available at

JONATHAN
FITZPATRICK

Made in the USA
Middletown, DE
13 December 2019